You're Wealthier Than You Think

How to Understand Money and Stop the Stress

Joseph Metzger

Copyright © 2021 Joseph Metzger

All rights reserved. No part of this work may be reproduced, distributed, or transmitted in any form or by any means, including photocopying, recording, or other electronic or mechanical methods, without the prior written permission of the author, except in the case of brief quotations embodied in critical reviews and certain other noncommercial uses permitted by copyright law.

Book design by Joseph Metzger.

Published by Metzger Publishing, Fairfax, Virginia, United States of America.
MetzgerPublishing@Gmail.com

Second printing edition 2021

To my wife and children,
whose love and inspiration
made this work possible.

CONTENTS

Introduction 1
Chapter 1: Setting Goals 5
    Setting general goals 8
    How does income impact your goal choices? 10
    Setting non-financial goals 11
Chapter 2: The Psychology of Finance 13
    How your personality influences your approach to money 13
    How culture affects your approach to money 16
    Money mistakes that have nothing to do with money 18
    Prosperity comes from doing the opposite of everyone else 21
    Money isn't everything 24
    Focus on the future, not the past 25
Chapter 3: Basic Tools 28
    Net Worth 29
    Income Statement 33
    Making a budget 36
    How do I track all this? 37

Chapter 4: How To Manage Debt 41
    Should I include a mortgage in this list? 47
    Optimizing interest rates 49
Chapter 5: How to Manage Cash 52
    Set up an emergency fund 53
    Don't set up an emergency fund 55
    Beyond the emergency fund 56
Chapter 6: Understanding Investment Accounts 58
    Taxable accounts 59
    Traditional retirement accounts 60
    Roth retirement accounts 65
    Health savings accounts 68
    Rollovers 70
    Roth conversions 72
    Which is better: the Roth IRA or the traditional IRA? 73
Chapter 7: Understanding Investments 76
    Bank accounts 79
    Bonds 81
    Stocks 82
    Mutual funds 84
    Exchange traded funds (ETFs) 86
    Options 86
    Residential real estate 88
    Commercial real estate 90
    Annuities 90
    Bitcoin and commodities 92

 Gold 93
 Don't be afraid! 94
Chapter 8: How to Choose Investments 98
 Avoid fixed income 99
 Understand your investments 100
 Stocks are usually the best choice 102
 Mutual funds as an alternate choice 109
 Leverage 111
Chapter 9: Minimizing Taxes 113
 For people with businesses 117
 For everyone 119
 Tax strategies that are not helpful 125
Chapter 10: The Importance of Saving 128
 Save money by cutting small expenses 130
 Save money by cutting large expenses 131
 Refocus your targeted spending levels 132
 But it's fun to spend money NOW! 135
 The other side of savings: income 138
 How much to save 140
 Your savings rate is more important than your investment return 141
Chapter 11: Cars 145
 Why do people like destroying themselves for a machine? 146
 How you should purchase cars 147
Chapter 12: Housing 152
 How to cut your housing expenses 153
 Buy or rent? 155

Home equity..160

Chapter 13: Insurance..164
    Auto insurance...169
    Homeowner's insurance..173
    Renter's insurance..175
    Title insurance...176
    Life insurance...179
    Garbage insurance (e.g., AFLAC and extended warranties)...........182
    Long-term care insurance..186
    Health insurance..190

Chapter 14: Credit Cards: Good or Evil?..197
    Getting started with credit..199
    If you choose to use credit...200

Chapter 15: Retirement...203
    Social Security..207
    Asset drawdown rates..209
    F.I.R.E – Good or evil?..213
    What if you achieve your goals early?...217

Chapter 16: Potpourri..224
    Two-Income Families vs. One-Income Families.............................224
    Credit Scores..228
    Don't lend money to friends and relatives.......................................231
    Charitable giving..233

About the Author..238

INTRODUCTION

A man is wandering the desert, dying of thirst. He comes across a small shop and begs the shopkeeper for water.

"I don't have any water," says the shopkeeper, "but perhaps you'd like a necktie?"

The man replies, "I'm dying of thirst. I don't need a necktie."

The shopkeeper says, "these are really nice neckties. They're 100% silk and hand stitched. You won't find a finer necktie anywhere. You really need one of these neckties."

"I DON'T WANT A NECKTIE," screams the man. "I WANT WATER!"

"Okay," says the shopkeeper. "There's a restaurant about three miles to the south from here."

The man disappears over a sand dune on his way to the restaurant. Four hours later he comes back to the shop, more tired and exhausted than before. "The restaurant won't let me in without a necktie."

It's really great to know what you want. Knowing what you want helps you to give yourself directions and goals in life. But sometimes what you want isn't always what you should want. Sometimes you don't even know what you want, or you don't have any idea how your goals and wants fit into the bigger picture of your life. That's where advice comes in, and this book is chock full of financial advice.

Once you get some advice, that's only half the battle. The other half is actually following the recommendations.

Several years ago, I had someone ask me if I thought he was financially ready to buy a house. He and I talked for a little while about his savings and income and some of the unexpected house expenses he might incur. After reviewing everything, I told him I thought he and his wife would be better off renting for another year and building up their savings and down payment first. Then I got a surprising response: "We already bought a house."

I learned right then that people who look for advice very often are seeking to validate something they did already. They're not interested in suggestions about what to do for the future; they just want you to tell them they're right.

So, let's get this out of the way: Everything you've done so far is right.

There.

If you're interested in learning more about personal finance, there's a lot to learn. I learn new things about finance almost every day, and I've been investing for nearly 30 years and working in the accounting and finance world for nearly 20. I've read a lot and seen a lot and talked with a tremendous number of people about their personal money issues.

It should come as no surprise, but everyone wants to be rich, to have enough money to do whatever he wants, to have time and flexibility, and, most important, not to have to worry about anything. Some people achieve this goal, but most don't.

There are nearly an infinite number of ways people's financial plans get derailed, and while it would be fun to list all of them (especially some of the less common reasons, such as trying to corner the silver market without an exit strategy, or sliding down a forty-foot razor blade), the good news is that it's not hard to find ways to get closer to your goals.

That is one of the amazing things about personal finance! This is not an all-or-nothing game, where you either live a life of ease and luxury, or you suffer an eternity like Sisyphus (but instead of pushing a boulder back to the top of a hill in perpetuity, you're busy returning shopping carts). There are numerous stages in between.

It might seem overwhelming when you think about the sheer volume of variables in finances and the amount there is to learn. It might seem overwhelming even to see the amount of information in this book.

But you don't have to do everything listed here; even if you get only two or three good ideas and add them to your financial plan, you can improve your finances a little bit, and if you can improve your finances a little bit, your life is going to be a little bit better. Or at least financially better. Finances can't fix everything in life, like making unhappy people become happy or giving you more hair, and if you ask my wife, no amount of personal finance expertise can fix all the things about me that annoy her so much. But better finances at least help with the money part of life, and that is a pretty big part.

The key for this is understanding money and the tools you can use to make money easier to handle. The key for understanding money is understanding yourself, the decisions you make, and why. Once you improve your understanding of yourself, you can begin to use the tools listed here to improve your finances and reduce your financial stress. Then you can focus on annoying your wife about things that don't involve money.

And that's precisely why you're wealthier than you think. You get to define yourself, you get to define your goals, and you get to define what wealth means to you. Combined with the application of time and planning, two things you control more than you realize, you can make anything happen.

This book doesn't have to be read directly from start to finish. It's okay just to pick out a chapter here or there on something you think could be interesting. There's no surprise at the end. The butler didn't do it. There's no secret meaning of life. You also shouldn't be intimidated just because finance is the topic and the numbers all have little dollar signs. The underlying principle of personal finance success is really easy: spend less than you earn, invest the difference, and apply time. That's it. The rest is just details.

CHAPTER 1:
SETTING GOALS

So you've decided you want to be rich. Great! But while "rich" generally relates to money, it also relates to how you want to live your life, and it doesn't mean the same thing to everyone. Let's look at three different people.

Bill has $500,000 per year of income from his job. The government takes $200,000. Bill really likes to buy stuff and consume. His $2 million house, 3 luxury cars, vacations, private school, and dining consume $350,000 per year. His wife spends and additional $100,000 per year, resulting in his $5 million debt growing by $150,000 per year.

Bill is "consumption rich." That's what most people think of when they think of "rich." They have lots of expensive possessions, a high annual income, and a fantastic lifestyle. Their Facebook page is the envy of all who behold it, and anyone who looks at it wonders why he can't be that successful too. In reality, their fantastic lifestyle is built on debt and is not sustainable without some drastic change, but that part is invisible on the outside. Their inevitable financial collapse hasn't happened yet, and Facebook doesn't have an option to post about events that haven't happened, with the exception of Doctor Who's Facebook page.

Fred earns $110,000 per year. His net worth is $2 million, but

$900,000 of that is in his house on which he has a $700,000 mortgage. Fred and his wife enjoy spending money, especially on their house, but they have enough self-discipline not to exceed their income. Their net worth generally grows each year along with their investments, but Fred has to continue working to support their lifestyle.

Fred has a high net worth, which makes him "asset rich." Having lots of money is great, but much of his net worth is tied up in his house, which doesn't produce any income and which consumes their cash flow for property taxes, mortgage payments, and maintenance. Fred doesn't have much time available for his own interests because he has to continue working to support his lifestyle, but at least he can tell people he's worth a lot of money.

Harry earns $50,000 per year from dividends on his $1.5 million investment portfolio, and he and his wife spend only $40,000 of that on a modest lifestyle. Harry and his wife spend their time with their friends, family, and hobbies doing whatever they want.

Harry is "time rich." This type of rich is almost invisible because Harry's outward consumption is so modest, and the commodity he has in the greatest supply, time, is invisible. Harry's Facebook page gets very few likes because nobody wants to look at pictures of someone who has lots of time. Nobody on the street is impressed when Harry drives his ten-year-old Toyota around. Although Harry can't consume as much as other people, he doesn't want much and he can do anything he wants without having to answer to anyone about how he spends his time (except his wife, who has a long list of chores for him which won't be finished until 30 years after he dies).

There are also combinations of these types of rich which include non-economic factors.

For example, Jerry might earn $200,000 per year, but he needs to work 90 hours per week, travelling 40 weeks per year, suffering tremendous pressure and stress, and being away from his family so much that his wife is practically a widow and his children orphans.

William, on the other hand, might earn $100,000 per year, but if he works only 30 hours per week from home at a job he enjoys and spends time with his family, is he less rich or more rich than Jerry? Who is the richest person in these examples?

The answer to that, of course, is a value judgment. Based on your lifestyle preferences, which could include how you want to spend your time, showing off vs. financial security, family obligations, enjoyment of work, or just being a miser, the answers differ. William might annoy his wife by being around her all the time and asking constantly what's for lunch, while Jerry might be such an obnoxious and horrible person that he would have gotten divorced long ago if not for the fact he was never around.

Or maybe William enjoys the family time and Jerry envies the time William has. Or maybe Jerry's kids are grown up and his wife is busy with her own career and there's nobody at home anyway. Or maybe Jerry's wife likes having privacy at home while her husband is travelling for work, which explains why Jerry's kids look like the mailman.

Much of personal finance is just that: personal (especially the bit about the mailman). You have to decide which type of rich you want to be, and what things are most important to you in life. Mathematically, of course, "consumption rich" is the hardest to achieve for the simple reason that your wealth requirements are the highest while your ability to accumulate wealth is hindered by your desire to consume it. "Time rich" is easiest to achieve if you have modest desires and a high propensity to save. All types of rich require time and effort.

There's nothing inherently wrong with any of these options. As long as you know where you're trying to go, you can make plans for how to get there.

I'll let you in on a little secret: If you find happiness in consumption, you're going to find yourself caught in a cycle called "hedonistic adaptation." That is, you'll be happy when you consume, but then you'll get used to it and you'll have to consume more to feel happy again, which you'll get used to, which then requires more consumption. There's no limit to this. The world is littered with examples of people who consumed vast amounts of wealth and ended up broke and unhappy.

Johnny Depp earned many millions of dollars over his career, but he also spent $300,000 per month on staff, $200,000 monthly on a private jet, $30,000 monthly on wine, and $75 million to buy 14 houses. He also went bankrupt. I suspect the high level of spending didn't result in much happiness for him.

Mike Tyson earned $400 million, and by the time he was 39, he was $40 million in debt. Perhaps he had fun spending $4.5 million on cars, $300,000 on two white Bengal tigers, and $2 million on a gold bathtub, but this probably didn't make him more happy as he walked into bankruptcy court.

"Consumption rich" is a fine goal, but it's also the most dangerous. You face a very high risk of failure and a very high probability that it won't make you more happy than being "asset rich" or "time rich."

Personally, I prefer "time rich" myself since I like control over my own destiny more than I like buying things or showing off on Facebook, but there are times when a white Bengal tiger sure could come in handy.

Setting general goals

Regardless of what wealth goals you choose, there are some general goals that help significantly to reduce your financial stress on your quest to achieve your long-term goals.

1. Have resources on hand so that emergencies are just an expense and not a source of financial anxiety. There's

nothing more unpleasant than having your two-year-old spill a milkshake on your laptop, except for not knowing how you'll pay for another laptop (or explaining to Mom why you gave a milkshake to a two-year-old).

2. Avoid peaks and valleys in your lifestyle. In economic terms, this is called "consumption smoothing," but in general terms, it means save when times are good so you can consume at the same rate when times are bad.

3. Build your net worth into income-producing investments so you have enough income to replace your labor. When you're young, your primary asset is your ability to work, and as you become older, you want to transition your primary asset from labor to capital so that your investments, instead of the sweat of your brow, provide for your needs.

4. Plan for your money to last for the rest of your life. The only thing scarier than dying is outliving your money.

Some people take the view that they should live for today. After all, there are no pockets in a shroud, and if you die without spending money, you'll never get the chance to enjoy the fruits of your labor.

If you have reason to believe you won't live long, this is an excellent approach to take. The reality for most people, though, is that you're going to live a long time, and if you don't plan ahead, living for today is going to make the future much more difficult and unpleasant for you. These four items are financial musts for everyone.

How does income impact your goal choices?

If you earn $350,000 per year, you obviously can make more choices than someone earning $35,000 per year. But if you earn $35,000 per year, there's no reason why you can't also have a financially secure and happy future.

First off, earning a high income is no guarantee of anything. If you earn $350,000 per year, you can mismanage your money and borrow until you're $3 million in debt, something that would be virtually impossible in the case of a lower-income household. If you combine massive debt with a divorce or business failure, you could end up in a financial hole from which you could never escape despite the high income.

Second, as with the question of what "rich" means, a high income doesn't do anything to guarantee happiness. All it guarantees is that you'll have more decisions to make and that you'll pay a lot of taxes.

From a mathematical standpoint, differences in income matter less and can be equalized through the application of time. A lower savings rate, but applied for more years and with more time for investment growth, is equal to a higher savings rate applied over a shorter time.

For example, if your goal is to retire on a tropical island drinking champagne every day, you can achieve that no matter what your income. If you earn $350,000 per year, you might be able to go to that island at age 40, whereas if you earn $35,000, you might have to work until you're 75.

Working until you're 75 might not be particularly appealing, but the addition of time to your financial plans can allow you to reach almost any goal. Time also gives you a chance to modify your goals. For example, you might decide a better end goal would be to retire in Nebraska drinking beer at age 60.

Either way, this all comes down to a question of personal choices, preferences, and tradeoffs. Nobody can tell you what the right answer is, but simply knowing that you have a choice and that you can achieve your goals with enough time can do wonderful things for your financial peace of mind.

Setting non-financial goals

It's worth noting that the main point of this book is setting financial goals and ways to achieve them, but along with deciding what type of rich you want to be, you also have to decide what your non-financial goals are in life.

If your only goal is to maximize your financial well-being, then what you have to do in your life is a simple math exercise: Work as hard as you can to grow your income, spend only the minimum amount needed to keep yourself alive, never get married or have children, never travel or have fun, and work until you die. Then you'd be able to leave a huge pot of money behind for the heirs you don't have.

Other than the most miserly people, almost nobody is going to choose this or recommend it (except for the government, perhaps, which would love for people to do nothing but generate a lifetime of tax revenue). There are lots of joys in life that come from sources other than money, for example:

- Getting married
- Having children
- Travelling
- Getting divorced
- Getting remarried

- Spending time with family and close friends

- Getting re-divorced
- Paying for your kids' weddings
- Paying for your kids' divorces

It's really up to you to decide what's most important in life, and it's not money. Of course, all the important things in life require money, so there's no getting out of managing your finances along with your life goals.

CHAPTER 2:
THE PSYCHOLOGY OF FINANCE

In some ways, money is more about psychology than math. The dollars and cents and ratios and returns are all mathematical, but that's not really the point of money. If you were stranded alone on a desert island, and a box washed ashore with $10 million in cash in it, what possible use would the money have? (It's worth noting that the IRS would consider this to be part of your worldwide, taxable income, and they would still find a way to take their taxes out of it. They would also avoid telling anyone where you are since that would violate taxpayer confidentiality).

Money has no value unto itself. It is simply a social tool that helps people to interact with each other more efficiently, to allocate resources among themselves, to incentivize certain behaviors, and to simplify tax collection. Like most human interactions, logic and math are rarely the first considerations in money decisions.

How your personality influences your approach to money

Different personality types have to approach money in different ways to achieve long-term financial success. Advice that works well for a person who's naturally inclined to save would work poorly for a person who enjoys spending impulsively. Think about your personality, and really be honest with yourself. "To thine own self be true," as Polonius said in Hamlet, much to the utter annoyance and boredom of high school kids since time immemorial. Were Polonius alive today, he probably also would have said, "wherefore suffereth I the slings and arrows of absent Facebook likes."

Whatever your financial-personality type is, it's unlikely you'll be able to change it very easily. Instead, when trying to apply the principles in this book, you'll need to think about them in the context of your own motivations and impulses so you can avoid fighting against yourself.

<u>The Spender</u>. This is the kind of person who enjoys buying stuff. Making a purchase is a thrill, whether it's a new Calphalon pot and pan set or a vacation to Mauritania. The Spender isn't opposed to planning for the future, but there's just so much great stuff to buy that the future isn't a priority. Besides, you can always start planning later.

Some Spenders are motivated to spend because they enjoy it for themselves. Other Spenders are motivated to spend because they want to impress other people with how much money they spent.

This is probably one of the most common personality types in the country, so if you're in this category, you have a lot of company. You can still succeed financially, even if you enjoy spending, but it'll be more of a challenge for you. The main things you'll have to ask yourself are:

- Am I spending money for something that will bring me happiness or just on impulse?
- Am I spending to impress other people? Are the people actually impressed, and is this making me happier?
- Can I derive as much happiness while spending smaller

amounts of money?

The Miser. This is the Ebenezer Scrooge type of person who values money for the sake of money, who rarely spends beyond the need for survival, and who loves to accumulate. Misers go beyond thrifty and into cheap. To illustrate the distinction, a thrifty person might save money by not ordering wine with his dinner, while a cheap person will drink some of the wine someone else ordered without offering to pay for it.

This personality type is exceedingly rare, but if you are a Miser, you'll have no trouble with finances in your life. However, you'll have lots and lots of other social problems, including periodic visits by Christmas ghosts. If you're happy with that, then good for you. If you're not happy, then you'll have to make some major changes in yourself which, unfortunately, go beyond the scope of personal finance.

The Saver. Like the Miser, the Saver is someone who values money more highly than acquisitions. The Saver feels a sense of security in having money, sometimes in the context of having a more secure future, and sometimes in the context simply of feeling more secure now against possible calamities. Unlike the Miser, however, the Saver is willing to spend money when appropriate (such as chipping in for his share of a dinner), and is willing to enjoy himself in moderation.

If you're a Saver, you'll probably manage your finances well. The main thing you can learn and improve on is some of the details and techniques to make your savings more efficient and effective so you can reach your goals faster and more easily.

The Unconcerned. An Unconcerned person isn't trying to spend money or to save money. If something interesting comes along, the

Unconcerned will spend money on it, and if nothing interesting comes along, the Unconcerned won't spend money. This personality type just isn't thinking about the future. This is also a fairly common trait among most people.

If you're in this category, the great news is that there's a lot you can do to improve your finances without a major psychiatric overhaul. Primarily, you'll need to learn how to think about the future and to put more value in the future than in the present.

You might need to make some changes in your present lifestyle to enable you to reach your long-term goals, but as long as spending money isn't compulsive for you, you should be able to make that change without too much difficulty.

Obviously, these personality types are the extremes, and there are many variations and subtleties in between. If you get a general idea of where you fit in and what your personality-based approach to money is, you'll have a much easier time figuring out how to apply the other principles in this book.

How culture affects your approach to money

You might be under the impression that you and your personality are the only things that impact how you choose to handle money, but there's also a tremendous amount of cultural influence that goes into the mix.

If you run out and buy a brand new, $100,000 Tesla, you can post pictures on Facebook, tell your friends and family how much you spent on your new car, and put on a very public display of your new purchase. Other people might ooh and ahh, give you likes, and post positive comments about how great your expensive purchase is.

Almost nobody would consider this showing off, and it's a good feeling when you can impress other people with what you did. Nobody will see that the car is leased and that you'll be making payments for the next five years for a car you won't ultimately own. You'll get an almost completely positive social response from your spending.

On the other hand, if you save for several years and build up $100,000 in your 401(k) plan, posting a picture of your retirement statement on Facebook will be attacked as boastful, unseemly, and a general taint on your character. People will feel resentful toward you for showing off how much money you saved, and they'll be jealous as well. The social response is going to be almost entirely negative.

Saving money is not going to get many likes.

In both cases, you're showing off $100,000, but in the consumption case you're applauded, and in the savings case you're attacked. Social status is judged by the amount of money you consume publicly on cars, houses, clothes, travel, and so forth, not by the amount of money you save or how well your investments perform.

The American culture is hardwired to reward consumption. It doesn't matter why the culture is this way; just accept that this is how it is, and that you can't change it any more than you can change your wife to stop complaining so much about how you shouldn't cook macaroni for seven minutes, even though you know from long experience that cooking it for eleven minutes like she prefers makes a soggy mess which everyone hates, except for her because she doesn't even eat the macaroni.

This is reinforced not just with social media, but with the advertisements that exist always and everywhere to persuade you that the next purchase you make is going to be the one that really makes you happy.

How many people in advertisements look unhappy because they spent too much money on the advertised product? How many ads encourage people not to spend money?

It makes sense; the advertisers make money only if they can persuade you that buying their product is great. They wouldn't advertise otherwise. Your financial future is not their concern (nor should it be anyone's concern but yours).

Banks also contribute to this, "helping" you with easy financing so you can make that purchase you really want now instead of waiting until later. They have wonderful, market-tested charts and ad copy to persuade you that the cost of financing is so low, you'd be missing out if you don't borrow. The banks, of course, make money only if you borrow. They have no reason to care about your financial future either.

Everywhere you look, people are trying to get you to make decisions that are pretty much the exact opposite of what you should be doing if you're going to be financially responsible. The pressure is enormous.

If you allow yourself to make decisions affecting your financial future based on cultural pressure, what have you accomplished? If you spend your retirement funds on an expensive car and clothes so you can impress strangers, it's hard to see how you've benefited yourself, your future, or even the people you impressed (unless you impressed a girl who's really pretty, in which case this is okay).

Money mistakes that have nothing to do with money

The culture isn't the only thing putting pressure on you to make financial mistakes. There are plenty of personal mistakes people make as well.

The biggest is marrying someone who doesn't share your financial goals and personality. Money is the number one cause of divorce in America. If a Saver marries a Spender, they'll be working toward conflicting goals, with the Saver resenting the Spender for squandering his labors, and the Spender resenting the Saver for stopping her from being happy.

That kind of a marriage might work in the long run, but it usually fails.

Understandably, people don't usually consider finances as part of the marriage decision, with notable exception of gold diggers who consider nothing but finances (well, maybe finances aren't the only thing gold diggers consider; besides wealth in a spouse, they probably are also looking for someone who is very old and very sick).

Going on a date and asking, "so, what's your net worth and credit score," is the kind of thing that probably results in not getting a second date. It's easier to ask the question later in a relationship, but if the answer is, "I'm $600,000 in debt from my master's degree in social work and I have $200,000 in credit-card debt from supporting my anime figurine obsession," ending the relationship after getting emotionally invested is more difficult.

Thus, most people choose not to ask about finances at all. But that's a major error. Divorce is an extremely disruptive and expensive process on your finances, and if you can reduce the odds of divorce right at the outset, that'll go a long way toward helping you to be more financially secure.

Whether you choose to ask at the beginning of the relationship at the risk of not getting more dates, or instead to ask later on and at the risk of losing your emotional investment, either way that loss is far less costly than a failed marriage.

Next is excessive concern with what other people think. You should make financial decisions that are right for you. Don't worry about what your friends and family think when they see you driving an old car or wearing clothes from Target. Don't concern yourself with what the neighbors might think if you don't renovate the kitchen. None of the people you impress is going to help you if you need money in the future. Nobody who admires your expensive car is going to help you retire when you get too sick to work.

If you try to play the game of impressing other people, you're going to lose. There's no limit to how much people can consume, and unless you're the wealthiest person in the world, there's always someone consuming more. Don't play the game.

Similarly, you should avoid coveting other people's possessions. The new car your friend bought might look great, but you have no idea what tradeoffs he made to buy it or what kind of damage he's doing to his financial future. Maybe he gave up a vacation to get the car. Maybe he's making only minimum payments on his debt. Maybe he cashed out his 401(k) and paid a huge penalty. The new car probably won't even add anything to his happiness within a few months, but all you'll remember is how happy he was when he bought the car.

The same thing applies to new phones, jewelry, houses, or anything else you see friends and family buying. If they decided the purchases were good for them, there's nothing wrong with that, but those were their choices and tradeoffs, not yours, and you shouldn't let them influence your spending decisions.

You'll probably find yourself looking upon other people's possessions with envy from time to time, despite your best efforts. That's just human nature. "Thou shalt not covet" was written in the Ten Commandments about 3,000 years ago. Very little has changed about people during that time, even if you might now covet your neighbor's iPhone instead of his goat. There's nothing wrong with being human, but you do have to acknowledge the influence it has on your choices.

Next, you should avoid letting pride get in the way of good decision making. For example, if you're without a job at a point in your life when you need income, it's okay to accept anything. Just because you have a master's degree in English doesn't mean you shouldn't drive for Uber or work with fast food while you look for a position in academia. Earning any money is better than earning nothing when you need money. Hurting yourself because a job isn't good enough for you doesn't make sense.

If you think you might be embarrassed if you don't buy some new gizmo or spend money on some activity that other people are spending money on, remember that it's okay not to spend the money. It's better to be embarrassed and wealthy than composed and poor.

Pride has no financial value. Spending money to maintain your pride does nothing to help your finances. If you choose to spend money to avoid a feeling of embarrassment, make sure you can afford it in the context of your long-term plans.

Prosperity comes from doing the opposite of everyone else

People like doing what's popular. There's a certain sense of comfort that comes with going along with a crowd. After all, if everyone is doing something, it's probably correct, otherwise everyone wouldn't be doing it.

The reality is that, financially at least, when everyone starts doing something, it's almost always wrong.

A really great company with great growth prospects could be a great investment at a given price, but as people rush to buy it, the price of the stock rises with no corresponding change in the underlying business, and eventually the price gets so high that it's no longer a good investment.

That was exactly what we saw during the Dot-Com bubble around the year 2000 as people bid up internet stocks to ridiculous levels, and then the whole thing came crashing down. Despite the fact that the internet really was transformative and actually exceeded the hype and expectations of the late 1990's, the rush of crowds and money into internet investments caused the prices to rise so high that the returns to investors were awful.

The same phenomenon happened with housing before the 2008 crash. Residential housing up to that point had a long history of rising in value consistently and being a safe investment for homeowners and banks. As was often pointed out, everyone needs a place to live and they're not making more land. Borrowing to buy a house was seen as the safest possible investment, and huge crowds of people and banks rushed to get in on the safe action.

Residential housing attracted so many people and so much capital that it rose in price to the point that it became a very poor investment for anyone who bought in at inflated prices, including the banking system which contributed the debt element and nearly collapsed in the process. That was despite the fact that people really do need places to live and nobody is making more land.

Even with something as mundane as a gas station, if you have a great location and make a lot of money, other people may see this and decide to open gas stations as well. In the process, they bid up the cost of land, construction, and equipment, and at the same time they create more competition for a fixed supply of business, at which point revenue drops for everyone and gas stations in that area become terrible investments.

This holds true for every investment in every area. As the investment generates good returns, more people crowd in, driving up costs, driving down revenue, and destroying the return to the investors. It doesn't matter how sound the underlying business premise is. Popular investments should be best avoided because the popularity ruins the investment.

Human nature, of course, makes it very hard to resist the siren song of easy success.

I know one man, a very nice person and otherwise very intelligent, who saw internet stocks rising rapidly in the late 1990's, and he decided it would be a great idea to borrow money on his credit card to buy internet stocks. That ended up quite badly for him when his stocks crashed and he was stuck with credit card debt.

A few years later, as housing prices began rising rapidly, that same man decided to start buying real estate, and he took out large loans on several properties. He even left his job to become a mortgage broker, and invited me to join him in his new venture that was sure to succeed.

Needless to say, I didn't follow him into that business. I also never heard from him again after the housing crash, but I can't imagine it he was happy with how things worked out.

During the latter part of 2017, as Bitcoin zoomed in price from $2,000 to $20,000, one person I know decided to borrow $10,000 on his credit card to invest in Bitcoin. Another person I know quit his job to become a Bitcoin broker, citing perpetually growing demand for this exciting new currency that would change the world. A third person I heard about borrowed his home equity to invest in Bitcoin.

Unlike the internet and housing (and even gas stations), there was no fundamental business underlying Bitcoin, and it lost 80% of its value in 2018. None of these people did particularly well by chasing trendy investment opportunities. Worse, even though Bitcoin eventually exceeded the $20,000 mark after a few years, they were wiped out because of the debt they took on with the initial investment.

This human instinct to chase after what everyone else is doing isn't limited just to money. If there are two lines at the DMV, one of which is very short and one of which is very long, people are often more inclined to wait in the long line on the assumption that everyone else in the line knows that the short line is for some other purpose and that to wait in that line would be folly. Nobody wants to ask if the other line can work and thus risk exposing their ignorance.

More commonly, with fashions, for example, people are inclined to dress the way other people dress, regardless of their own preferences, for fear of looking out-of-the-ordinary. That had some rather catastrophic results in the 1970's, if you're ever inclined to look at some old pictures.

And with consumption, if everyone in your social circle is taking trips to Europe, enjoying gourmet meals, living in grandiose homes, and purchasing new cars, the natural human instinct is to do the same thing. The potential catastrophic result in that case is that you destroy your financial future in the process of trying to fit in.

This is not an easy instinct to overcome. The best option is generally to limit your social circle to people who share your views on money and consumption, preferably toward the side of consuming less, but obviously there's a limit to how much you can control this.

In general, as long as you remember that what other people are doing is probably wrong and you avoid the temptation to go along with whatever seems trendy, you increase significantly your odds of financial prosperity.

Money isn't everything

Although money is an extremely important part of life, maximizing wealth isn't everything. Having more money can help you become more happy when you're starting out from nothing, but once you've met your basic needs, additional money and a more expensive lifestyle generally won't improve your happiness all that much.

Going from homeless to having an apartment provides a huge boost in happiness that's long lasting. Going from famine to having food gives another huge boost. Having a car vs. no car, a phone vs. no phone, or internet vs. no internet also provides a huge boost in happiness.

But going from a Toyota to a Lexus has a much smaller boost. Increasing your home from 2,000 square feet to 3,000 square feet has a smaller boost, and moving from a 7,000 square-foot home to an 8,000 square-foot home has almost no impact on your happiness at all.

The more you consume, the less benefit you get from additional consumption.

If you can avoid the temptation to allow your lifestyle to become more expensive as your wealth grows, you'll have the opportunity to drive more surplus cash flow into investments in your own future. Over time, once your capital base becomes large enough, you'll have enough money to fund your lifestyle in perpetuity, at which point additional money and investment has even less utility on your happiness.

Watching your investments grow from $0 to $10,000 is very exciting since it represents a real cushion in the case of unexpected events. Growing from $10,000 to $100,000 is exciting since you have significant capital available if you need it. Growing from $100,000 to $1 million adds to the happiness of knowing that your financial future is becoming more secure. But growing from $1 million to $3 million just adds more cushion and more options, which is nice, but not as exciting. When your net worth grows from $3 million to $10 million, the amount of additional happiness in your life is probably less than what you gained when you saved your first $10,000 (although I'd still rather have $10 million than $3 million).

If you don't allow your lifestyle costs to grow to infinity, then eventually you get to the point that additional money has no more utility. When there's no longer anything you can do with money that adds to your happiness significantly, there's nothing wrong with spending your time and effort on non-financial things, like friends, family, and hobbies.

This is a problem most people don't have, of course, but it can be really eye opening to realize that money has its limits, just like everything else in life.

Focus on the future, not the past

As you work toward reaching the limit of what money can do for your happiness, there are a lot of decisions you'll have to make. As you learn more about money management, you'll probably also have a lot of regrets about some poor decisions you made in the past.

Many people borrow way too much money for an expensive college with a non-productive major, or they borrow too much on credit cards at high interest rates to buy junk, or they overspend on cars, housing, and travel, or they invest poorly and lose lots of hard-earned capital.

Mistakes are plentiful in life for everyone. Don't beat yourself up about them. Everyone makes mistakes.

As long as you learn something from your mistakes, consider the losses to be the cost of an education for doing better in the future.

There's no benefit in giving yourself stress about the past. If you have a massive debt, spend your time trying to figure out how to handle it as efficiently as possible. If you bought a house or a car that's more expensive than you can really afford, decide whether or not it makes sense to sell the house or car and buy something cheaper. If you put money into an investment that does poorly, or something irrevocable like an annuity, just accept it, and figure out how to manage your finances based on where you are now, not based on how things could have been.

In economics, there's something called "sunk costs." That's money you put into something in the past, and which you can't get back. People, often smart people or people running businesses, make the mistake of assuming that because they have a sunk cost from an old decision, therefore they have to keep putting more money into supporting the same thing.

Sunk costs are gone. If you did something in the past that no longer makes sense, putting more money into it in order to justify yourself doesn't make sense either, but people do that frequently.

For example, if you invested $100,000 in your business, but it's losing money every month and nothing can change that, it's better to go out of business than to keep putting more cash into it. If you bought a car and you can't afford the payments, it's better to sell the car and pay off the debt than to keep getting into a deeper financial hole. If you are halfway through a master's degree in social work practices of the 19th century, it's better to drop out rather than pouring more money into a worthless degree.

Cut your losses and move on. Not only do decisions from the past not have any bearing on what you should do now, but you shouldn't even think about them or what you should have done differently.

Thinking about what could have been serves only to make you miserable. Thinking about what could be gives you hope.

CHAPTER 3:
BASIC TOOLS

It's great to know where you want to end up financially, much the same way it's great to know where you want to go on vacation. The destination is important, but so too is how you get there. I know I'd like to go to Disney World. That's the destination. Then I have to decide: Do I want to fly there or drive there? Once I arrive, do I want to be gouged by in-the-park hotel prices, or would I rather be gouged by parking fees when I arrive from out of the park?

Would I rather buy a bunch of $12 hot dogs and $6 sodas for my family, or should I study techniques for smuggling in outside food and drinks? Is it better to wait in line for three hours for Space Mountain or three hours at Big Thunder Mountain? There's a lot of decision making that goes into achieving your vacation goals.

If you decide that your financial goal is to be rich, and once you decide exactly what you mean by "rich," there's a lot of decision making that goes into reaching your financial goal. The same way that you'd plan a vacation by using various travel websites and apps, you need some basic tools for financial planning as well. Or you could leave both the vacation and the financial plan all up to your spouse and hope everything gets planned well, and if it doesn't work out the way you want, just complain a lot.

Net Worth

You can't get where you want if you don't know where you are. That's where a net worth statement comes in.

Your net worth is simply what you own minus what you owe. It's the barometer that tells you whether you're rich or bankrupt (and that's a lot more exciting than a real barometer, which, come to think of it, is probably one of the least exciting tools ever invented in the entire history of mankind).

The things you own are "assets." Those include savings accounts, retirement accounts, real estate, gold, stolen Nazi art, and Beanie Babies (I'm still waiting for the prices to come back).

I don't consider cars to be assets even though they have value. Car ownership hurts you financially. Unless you drive for Uber, cars don't generate income for you. Instead, they consume money for car payments, insurance payments, tax payments, gasoline, repairs, registration fees, and maintenance. Car ownership also has a nasty habit of attracting friends who need rides to the airport, while truck ownership attracts friends who need help moving. Cars are a financial drain, and if you think of a car as an asset, it's easy to trick yourself into buying more car than would be appropriate.

However, if you want to list a car as an asset, especially if you're considering selling it as a way to improve your cash on hand or to reduce debt, that's okay. Just be careful.

What you owe is called a "liability." That includes things like mortgages, credit-card debt, student loans, car loans, and court judgments against you for personal cash advances on your company credit card that you lost playing blackjack at the Foxwoods Casino in Mashantucket, Connecticut on New Year's Eve 2010 and then lied about. No, that wasn't me. Yes, that really did happen to an employee I had to deal with.

There are all sorts of ways to accumulate liabilities besides getting caught embezzling company funds at a casino. Sometimes it's through no fault of your own, such as medical debt. Sometimes it's because of a sin of omission, such as forgetting to pay your car insurance bill and then having an accident. Other times it's because of a sin of commission, such as spending more than you can afford to try and impress a girl.

Generally speaking, the sins of commission are more fun than the sins of omission, otherwise you wouldn't do them, but whether or not you had fun getting into debt doesn't really matter. You can address the how-you-ended-up-in-debt question as you plan for the future and decide how much fun you can really afford. What matters is what you owe.

Here is a sample net worth statements to give you an idea what this looks like:

Milton Solvent
Net Worth
February 11, 2020

Assets

Checking	$3,500
Savings	$14,000
Investments	$25,000
Retirement	$75,000
House	$395,000
Total Assets:	**$512,500**

Liabilities

Mortgage	$336,000
Credit card bill	$7,400
Student loans	$85,000
Car loan	$22,500
Casino cash advance	$0
Total Liabilities:	**$450,900**

Net Worth	**$61,600**

Milton Solvent has a positive net worth of $61,600. He has some debts, but he's starting to grow his savings and investments, and he has more money than he owes. This is known as "solvent," which is very convenient since that happens to be Milton's name. It's also where you want to be.

Of course, not every balance sheet is good.

Casino Cash Advance Boy
Net Worth
February 11, 2020

Assets	
Checking	$1,500
Savings	$500
Investments	$0
Retirement	$5,000
House	$0
Total Assets:	**$7,000**

Liabilities	
Mortgage	$0
Credit card bill	$17,500
Student loans	$112,000
Car loan	$33,000
Casino cash advance	$3,611
Total Liabilities:	**$166,111**

Net Worth	**-$159,111**

Casino Cash Advance Boy owes money for all sorts of things, except a house because he couldn't get approved for a mortgage due to the court judgments against him for the casino cash advance. He also has minimal assets, which leaves him owing $159,111 more than he has. That's known as "insolvent."

It's not uncommon for people to be insolvent, especially if they're young and starting life with lots of student-loan debt. That's obviously not where you want to be in the long run, especially as you get older, but it's okay to start there.

The good news is that older people generally have a higher net worth than younger people. That comes from the basic fact of having had longer to earn money, save, invest, and pay down debt. According to a 2016 Federal Reserve survey, the median net worth in the U.S. by age is:

Age	Median Net Worth
Under 35	$11,100
35-44	$59,800
45-54	$124,200
55-64	$187,300
65-74	$224,100
75+	$264,800

Ideally, as you get older, you want your net worth to rise so high that you can live off income generated from your assets without having to work. What that age should be and whether or not you wish to stop working are personal decisions, but failure to maintain the solvency of your net worth will force you to work longer whether you want to or not, and it will lead to unnecessary stress in your life.

A sufficiently insolvent person might also be forced into bankruptcy. Fortunately, we don't live in a Charles Dickens dystopia where you'll end up in debtor's prison until you make good on your debts, but bankruptcy makes life much more difficult. It's always better having more options rather than fewer.

If your bottom line net worth isn't what you hoped it would be at this point in your life, or if you're insolvent, don't fret. The rate at which and the direction in which your net worth is moving can provide hope. If your net worth is falling, though, then you should most definitely fret. I'm not sure how one goes about fretting, but that's what you should do until you stop the problem from getting worse.

Income Statement

Your income statement tells you whether your net worth is rising or falling. It's the infamous "bottom line" that big, important corporate people are always talking about, usually loudly into their cell phones while you're trying to enjoy a meal at a restaurant.

The first thing on an income statement is obviously "income," things that provide money to you, for example, salary from a job, net profit from side work, dividends, Social Security, interest (applicable only in ancient history museums since it's so minimal these days), trust fund distributions, and a nickel you pick up off the street.

Income does not include money you borrow. Taking out a personal loan or a student loan or a home-equity loan does not improve your financial position, because the cash you collect is equal to the cash you owe. Never consider money you borrow to be income available for spending.

The other part of the income statement is "expenses," or things that consume your money, such as housing, insurance, food, entertainment, keeping your spouse happy, travel, vaccines for your children, alimony to your first wife, alimony to your second wife, the legal fees for the divorce from your current spouse whom you failed to keep happy, wedding expenses for your upcoming marriage, the bill for the psychiatrist you really should be visiting, and the chiropractor bill for hurting your back after picking up a nickel off the street.

Income minus expenses is your "net income." If this number is positive, it means you have money left over every month and your net worth is growing. If it's negative, it means you're spending more money than you earn and you're heading toward bankruptcy.

Other than for occasional, short periods of time, such as an annual vacation, a major car repair, or a home renovation, you want your income statement to be positive.

It's worth noting that, from a technical accounting standpoint, "expenses" are a term distinct from "cash flow." For example, a mortgage payment, which includes an interest portion and a debt-repayment portion, would have the finance charge or interest listed on your income statement as an expense, while the principal portion would be listed on your balance sheet as debt reduction. An extra credit-card payment wouldn't be on your income statement at all since it's not related to a finance charge and the reduction in your cash would be exactly offset by a reduction in your debt.

You can make this really complicated if you want to, but you don't have to be an accountant. For most people, it's best to keep it simple. Look at where your money is going and don't bother with making your basic financial reports compliant with all accounting rules. If you're really interested in learning about accounting details, there are many great textbooks available on that subject, or, instead of reading textbooks, you could save time and just take a Unisom.

For someone getting started on an income statement, I recommend just treating all debt payments as expenses and making life easy.

Here are sample income statements to give you an idea of what these look like:

Milton Solvent
Income Statement
February 29, 2020

Income
Salary	$5,000.00
Side work	$500.00
Dividends	$250.00
Interest	$0.01
Total Income:	**$5,750.01**

Expenses
Mortgage	$1,605.00
Utilities	$300.00
Credit card bill	$250.00
Student loans	$515.00

Car payment	$400.00
Gasoline	$75.00
Food	$500.00
Insurance	$175.00
Entertainment	$275.00
Cell phone	$195.00
Total:	**$4,290.00**

Net Income	**$1,460.01**

Casino Cash Advance Boy
Income Statement
February 29, 2020

Income

Salary	$4,100
Side work	$0
Dividends	$0
Interest	$0
Total:	**$4,100**

Expenses

Rent	$1,400
Utilities	$275
Credit card bill	$350
Student loans	$600
Car payment	$550
Gasoline	$150
Food	$750
Insurance	$225
Alimony wife 1	$450
Alimony wife 2	$195
Total:	**$4,945**

Net Income	**-$845**

As before, Milton Solvent is doing much better than Casino Cash Advance Boy. Milton is working harder to earn more income, he's spending less money, and he has savings left over at the end of the month.

Casino Boy is earning less money and spending more, so much so that he's losing $845 every month. That loss either reduces his assets or it grows his debt, both of which are bad. He really needs to change something before he reaches his financial doom.

Unlike a net worth statement, which is fairly straightforward, the income statement has a little more judgment involved for what you include. Is it worth listing groceries separate from dining out? Should you list auto insurance separate from life insurance? Should you list your credit-card payments individually or as a group?

The answer: Do whatever makes the most sense to you. If it helps to use more detail, that's fine. If you prefer to group things together more broadly to make it easier, that's fine too. The important thing is to make sure you list everything you actually spend money on so you know whether your finances are getting better or worse.

Making a budget

This is one of the easier reports to make. Take your income statement, and if you're satisfied with the net income, there's your budget! If you're not satisfied with the net income, consider making some changes to reduce your planned expenses. For example, you might see that your spouse spends a lot of money on dining out during work, and you might aim to reduce that. Or perhaps your spouse spends too much on clothes and accessories, and you might reduce that instead. Maybe your spouse's car is too expensive and should be traded in for a cheaper, older model.

Surely there's something your spouse spends money on that you can cut. You could also consider cutting some of your own expenses, but most likely your own expenses are well thought out and necessary, and anyway it's easier to blame someone else for the overspending.

Obviously, the step of judging the value of your various spending categories and amounts is highly personal and not always so easy. For married couples, when you start attacking each other over who spends what, you tread into dangerous territory. But for your long-term financial health, this is something you have to work through.

While you're making your budget, I also highly recommend you include line items for things you don't always spend money on, but which are highly likely, for example, car repairs, home repairs, planned vacations, or medical expenses.

To do that, take a look at what you spent on those in the past year. If you spent $3,000 on car repairs, budget $250 per month for repairs. If you spent $6,000 fixing your home, budget $500 per month for home repairs. If your vacation cost $6,000 and your medical costs were $1,200, budget $500 monthly for vacations and $100 monthly for medical costs.

Many people find it easier to take this budget for things on which they didn't spend money and put it into a savings account to reduce the temptation to consider it extra money available for spending. Other people are content to leave it in checking or elsewhere. As long as you're setting aside a reserve for these predictable, but irregular expenses, it doesn't matter which option you choose.

With what's left over at the end of your budgeting process, make sure you save it. Don't go through a budgeting exercise and use it as an excuse to spend more.

How do I track all this?

There are just as many techniques for tracking your finances as there for ruining them. Here are a few basic options:

<u>Multiple bank accounts</u>. This is probably one of the most common tools people use. Your income goes into a checking account, and your

expenses come out of it. Money you're saving for emergencies, car repairs, or college goes into a separate account for each purpose. Retirement accounts hold investments, and if you have money left over in your checking account at the end of the month, that gets moved into a savings account.

This technique has the advantage of being the easiest to understand and the easiest to manage. You don't have to think much, and if changing your behavior is a challenge, this one is the easiest ways to get used to saving for different priorities.

As long as you see your balances generally going up each month, and as long as you have money left over to move into savings every month, you're going in the right direction.

The major downside to this is that you never really know exactly how fast your progress is, if you're saving enough, or what kinds of changes you should make if your balances aren't growing. However, opening up multiple accounts is far better than doing nothing, and this technique will help you more than it will hurt.

As an side, some people use a variation on this where they keep cash in separate envelopes for separate purposes (e.g., have an envelope for groceries, an envelope for rent, an envelope for insurance, etc.). This variation is far less secure than using bank accounts since you run the added risk of losing physical money, and I don't recommend it.

Spreadsheets. Whether you keep your money in one account or in multiple account, spreadsheets are a step up in the organization process. They give you much more flexibility to track your income and expenses in detail, and they make it much easier to see your progress over time.

This requires, of course, that you're comfortable with spreadsheets and that you're disciplined enough to keep it up to date, at least monthly, with all your activity. If you choose this route, you have maximum flexibility for how you put together your reports and track your data, which is both a blessing and a curse.

When you go to a movie theater and there's only one seat left, it's really easy to know where to sit. When you go into an empty theater, the choice of a seat is much more difficult. Worse yet, when you finally pick a seat, and someone comes along and says, "excuse me sir. This theater is reserved seating and you're in my seat," you run a high risk of spilling your popcorn or soda as you try to move to an unreserved seat (although if you can manage to spill your popcorn and soda on the other guy's seat first, that's at least a bonus).

So too with spreadsheets: The choice of how to set it up is vast, and the odds of tracking things incorrectly are higher than with other tools.

Personal finance software. This is the preferred method. Personally, I like Quicken, but other people use Mint.com or other apps for tracking their finances. Ideally, you want something that organizes your accounts, does all the math, and is able to download transactions directly from your bank so that you don't have to do all the data entry or tracking.

You'll still have to invest time in getting everything set up initially, and you'll still have to invest time to make sure your records are up to date. I would suggest making that effort at least weekly, but updating your accounts monthly would be the minimum.

The big benefit to personal finance software is that the structure is already laid out for you, and that includes pre-made reports that simplify greatly the task of tracking your progress or identifying things you might need to change (or more likely, that your spouse needs to change).

The downside is that good personal finance software is generally not free, and it generally has a learning curve involved in understanding what the software does.

Whatever option you choose, I recommend strongly that 1) you invest the time and effort to learn how to use it effectively, and 2) you invest the time and effort to keep it up to date. Unfortunately, there's no shortcut available here, and getting your finances organized is going to require time and effort. But if you make that investment, the payoff is going to be more financial freedom in the future and far less stress.

CHAPTER 4:
HOW TO MANAGE DEBT

Once upon a time, there was a magical fairy named Blanco De Blanc who accumulated mountains of credit-card debt while purchasing anime figurines. She couldn't help herself, and she bought every figurine should could find, despite the 27.99% interest rate on her credit card.

After a few years, she owed $128,000 for the figurines plus $97,000 in accumulated interest. Using her magic fairy calculator, she realized it would take 62 years to pay off her debt if she made only minimum payments, and this would be possible only if she stopped buying figurines.

Blanco De Blanc took her magic wand, waived it, and with a shower of sparkles and light, she conjured a paid-off credit card bill. She lived happily ever after.

If you're like Blanco De Blanc at running up debt, you probably wish you had a magic wand like hers. Although we don't live in a fairy-tale world, there is an actual type of magic wand just like hers. The only difference is that the real-world magic wand, instead of being an enchanted stick, is made up of self-discipline, metaphor, and math. It doesn't have sparkles or light, and it's also really slow. And it's not magic. And it's really more of a technique than a wand. And there are two of them.

Or three, if you include debt awareness reduction, which basically involves ignoring your debt and hoping it goes away. Or four if you include debt increasing techniques.

Okay, so getting rid of debt isn't at all like a magic wand. The point is that you can make your debt go away.

There are two main techniques for debt reduction: the mathematically-optimized way, and the psychologically-optimized way. Both options work, and both options require the same thing before you even start: Spend less money than you earn so that you have capital left over for reducing your debt balances.

You don't have to have a lot of extra money to put toward debt reduction. Even $5 per month speeds up the process more than $0 per month, although obviously more is better. The main thing is that you're not making things worse by continuing to take on more debt, and that your allocating extra money each month toward paying your debt off faster.

<u>Mathematically-optimized technique</u>. This is my preferred way for getting out of debt as quickly as possible.
1. Make a list of all your debts and the interest rates.
2. Sort the list from the highest interest rate to the lowest interest rate.
3. Make minimum payments on all debts. Missing a payment on anything can trigger penalty interest rates and reduce your access to credit, both of which are going to set you back.

4. Determine how much extra money you have available to apply toward debt reduction, and send all of it toward the highest-rate debt first.

5. Once the highest-rate debt is paid off, apply the full payment from that debt, plus your additional payments, and add them to the payment on your next-highest-rate debt.
6. Once that's paid off, apply that full payment to the next-highest-rate debt, and continue until all the debt is paid off.

The advantage of this technique is that it minimizes your interest expense and gives you the fastest exit out of debt. Here's an example of what this looks like for Billy McWasteful, who owes quite a lot of money:

Billy McWasteful's Outstanding Debts

Account	Amount	Interest Rate	Minimum Payment
Visa card	$26,500	27.99%	$722
MasterCard	$5,000	12.99%	$91
Honda loan	$22,500	8.90%	$361
Toyota loan	$10,500	4.90%	$148
Student loan	$85,000	4.60%	$542
Total	$149,500		$1,864

Billy sorted his debts from highest-rate to lowest-rate. He realized it would take twenty years to get out of debt completely if no additional payments were made. Getting into debt is easy, but twenty years to get out is a really long time, so Billy decides to pay an extra $500 per month.

Mathematically, it should be applied first to his Visa Card, which has the highest interest rate at 27.99%. His first payments would thus be:

STEP 1: Billy McWasteful's Extra Payment

Account	Amount	Interest	Minimum	Additional	Total

		Rate	Payment	Payment	Payment
Visa card	$26,500	27.99%	$722	$500	$1,222
MasterCard	$5,000	12.99%	$91	$0	$91
Honda loan	$22,500	8.90%	$361	$0	$361
Toyota loan	$10,500	4.90%	$148	$0	$148
Student loan	$85,000	4.60%	$542	$0	$542
Total	$149,500		$1,864	$500	$2,364

Paying off that first debt is always hardest. Even with the extra payment, it would take Billy thirty months to pay off his Visa card due to the extremely high interest rate, but Billy pushes forward.

Once the Visa card is finally paid off, Billy has the $1,222 payment available, and he doesn't spend it on a new car. Instead, he adds it to his Mastercard payment.

STEP 2: Billy McWasteful's Extra Payment

Account	Amount	Interest Rate	Minimum Payment	Additional Payment	Total Payment
~~Visa card~~	~~$0~~	~~27.99%~~	~~$0~~	~~$0~~	~~$0~~
MasterCard	$3,675	12.99%	$91	$1,222	$1,313
Honda loan	$15,871	8.90%	$361	$0	$361
Toyota loan	$7,087	4.90%	$148	$0	$148
Student loan	$77,991	4.60%	$542	$0	$542
Total	$149,500		$1,864	$500	$2,364

Billy's total monthly debt payments remain the same at $2,364, but now he's paying $1,313 per month to his MasterCard instead of $91. He can fly through his payments to his MasterCard in only three months at this rate! When that's paid off, he moves on to his next debt, the Honda loan:

STEP 3: Billy McWasteful's Extra Payment

Account	Amount	Interest	Minimum	Additional	Total

Account	Amount	Interest Rate	Minimum Payment	Additional Payment	Total Payment
~~Visa card~~	~~$0~~	~~27.99%~~	~~$0~~	~~$0~~	~~$0~~
~~MasterCard~~	~~$0~~	~~12.99%~~	~~$0~~	~~$0~~	~~$0~~
Honda loan	$15,171	8.90%	$361	$1,313	$1,674
Toyota loan	$6,746	4.90%	$148	$0	$148
Student loan	$77,293	4.60%	$542	$0	$542
Total	**$99,210**		**$1,051**	**$1,313**	**$2,364**

Billy now adds his $1,313 payment from his MasterCard to his Honda Payment, and the pesky Honda payment is gone in 9 months! From there:

STEP 4: Billy McWasteful's Extra Payment

Account	Amount	Interest Rate	Minimum Payment	Additional Payment	Total Payment
~~Visa card~~	~~$0~~	~~27.99%~~	~~$0~~	~~$0~~	~~$0~~
~~MasterCard~~	~~$0~~	~~12.99%~~	~~$0~~	~~$0~~	~~$0~~
~~Honda loan~~	~~$0~~	~~8.90%~~	~~$0~~	~~$0~~	~~$0~~
Toyota loan	$5,593	4.90%	$148	$1,674	$1,822
Student loan	$74,938	4.60%	$542	$0	$542
Total	**$80,531**		**$690**	**$1,674**	**$2,364**

The $1,674 Honda payment then gets applied to the Toyota payment, which goes away in three months. Finally:

STEP 5: Billy McWasteful's Extra Payment

Account	Amount	Interest Rate	Minimum Payment	Additional Payment	Total Payment
~~Visa card~~	~~$0~~	~~27.99%~~	~~$0~~	~~$0~~	~~$0~~
~~MasterCard~~	~~$0~~	~~12.99%~~	~~$0~~	~~$0~~	~~$0~~
~~Honda loan~~	~~$0~~	~~8.90%~~	~~$0~~	~~$0~~	~~$0~~
~~Toyota loan~~	~~$0~~	~~4.90%~~	~~$0~~	~~$0~~	~~$0~~
Student loan	$74,145	4.60%	$542	$1,822	$2,364
Total	**$74,145**		**$542**	**$1,822**	**$2,364**

Billy then applies the full $2,364 toward his student loan and wipes it out in 33 months. Altogether, that extra $500 monthly payment cut Billy's time in debt from 20 years down to a little over 6 ½ years. He did this while maintaining the same monthly payment the whole time, and when he finally climbed out of the debt hole, he found himself with an additional $2,364 left over each month for savings, retirement, investments, or any other priority.

The key for making this work is threefold: Set aside money each month for extra debt payments, don't borrow more money, and when you pay off a debt, don't spend your monthly payment on new stuff!

That goes double for when you pay off all your debts. Keep making your same payments, but save and invest the money in yourself for your future; don't spend it all now, and, please, don't go back into debt.

<u>Psychologically-optimized technique</u>. Some people get frustrated as they try to pay off debt. They make payments each month, but the debts don't go away very quickly, which can lead to a sense of disappointment and which can cause people to give up trying.

If you need to see individual payments disappear more quickly to give yourself a psychological boost, all you have to do is change step 1. Simply sort your debts from smallest to largest and apply your extra payment to the smallest debt first.

The rest of the process is exactly the same.

Using Billy's example, if he were to add his extra payment to his smallest debt, the MasterCard, he would see his first debt disappear in only nine months. Mathematically, this results in more interest payments over the course of paying off all the debts, and the final payoff will take 6 months longer to reach.

There are some people who insist that the only debt-payoff

method that is acceptable is the mathematically-optimized way, and there are other people who insist that the psychologically-optimized way is the only option. In reality, either option is better than doing nothing, and the option that makes it easiest for you to stick to the plan is the one you should choose.

And one note about minimum payments: Make sure they actually cover the finance charges.

During the housing boom and ending by 2009, there was something called a "negative amortization mortgage," in which the payments you made were actually less than the accrued interest, and in which the mortgage balance increased each month. The theory behind this was that housing prices would rise forever, and you'd come out ahead by letting your debt grow, but that theory was about as sound as the idea of building prosperity through the sale of $100 bills at $97 each.

Thankfully that kind of mortgage is very rare now, and minimum payments are almost always in excess of finance charges, but if you ever see something like that offered, run away! Or refer your worst enemy to that bank.

Should I include a mortgage in this list?

There's some debate among personal-finance experts about whether or not to include a mortgage in your debt list.

Mortgage debt is generally long-term with a low interest rate. Paying off your mortgage faster is equivalent to getting a small, but guaranteed return on investment equal to your interest rate.

Does it make sense to commit cash to a low-return investment, or is it better to invest the cash in something higher-yielding like stocks? If you're starting out, don't worry about paying off the mortgage faster. You have lots of other obligations to deal with first, and since the mortgage is generally your largest debt and also your cheapest debt, it'll likely come at the bottom of your debt-payoff list regardless of how you sort it.

When you reach the point that extra mortgage payments are an option, I recommend including it in your debt list and paying it off faster.

Investing the extra mortgage payments in stocks is typically going to make your net worth grow faster, and mathematically that makes sense since stocks usually grow faster than mortgage interest. But from a cash flow standpoint, a higher net worth doesn't automatically help you write that monthly mortgage check (checks are a metaphor, of course; other than an occasional birthday present, I can't recall the last time I used a check for something).

You can't make debt payments by pulling bricks out of your house, and selling stocks to pay your mortgage is painful during times when stocks are down, even if the number for your net worth is higher in the process.

However, once that mortgage is paid off, your monthly cash flow is dramatically improved and greatly increases the flexibility you have to invest more without stress, retire early, deal with unforeseen challenges, or pursue other interests.

Personally, I believe that extra peace of mind that comes from having a paid-off mortgage is more valuable than having a higher net worth, but there's nothing wrong if you prefer to invest your extra mortgage payments instead.

The only option that's bad: spending the money. Unfortunately, human nature being what it is, people who intend to take extra money and invest it instead of paying down the mortgage often increase their spending instead, which is financially destructive. Paying down the mortgage removes the temptation to spend, and a small, safe return is better than making the money go away.

Optimizing interest rates

Some debts have usurious interest rates, like the Visa card at 27.99% that Billy McWasteful ran up. In Billy's example, he tackled the debt as is, but there's no reason to accept a high interest rate just because you have it already.

Some credit cards will give you a better interest rate if you simply call up and ask for a better rate. If you cut your rate from 27.99% down to 15% or 3%, all of that interest saved can go directly toward reducing your balance instead of padding the bank's revenue. There's no reason not to ask. The worst thing that can happen is the bank will tell you, "no." They're not going to get angry and raise your rate or get offended and blab to all your friends how you're not paying them back fast enough. You'd be surprised how often a bank will accommodate a polite request.

You can also try calling the issuing banks of your other credit cards with no balances. They might offer promotional balance-transfer rates that are appealing. The balance transfer often comes with a fee of 3% or 4%, but if you cut your interest rate from 27.99% down to 3% for a year, it's worth paying the transfer fee. If you're feeling really adventurous, and assuming your idea of an adventure involves math and paperwork, you might consider opening a new credit card with a promotional balance-transfer rate.

However, before opening a new credit line, you have to be honest with yourself about how likely you are to use the new credit line to save on interest vs. running up new debt. If you know that you like to spend or that temptation is hard to resist, you're better off paying the higher interest rather than making the problem worse.

If you own a home with equity, you could also consider getting a home equity line of credit (HELOC) and using that to pay off your other debts. The HELOC generally has lower rates than almost any debt, except a primary mortgage, and it comes with tremendous liquidity and flexibility. HELOCs are generally quite easy to get and use, but as with opening any new credit line, make sure you're not going to be tempted to renovate the kitchen and get back into debt once the credit cards are paid off.

Spending is far more dangerous and damaging to your financial future than paying a higher interest rate from the outset.

If you have a mortgage, you might consider refinancing the mortgage and rolling your other debts into it to take advantage of the lower interest rate. You might consider refinancing even if you don't have other high-interest loans to roll into it.

The decision on whether or not to refinance a mortgage is a fairly straightforward one: Is the new interest rate lower than the old interest rate? If it is and there's a big difference in rates, refinance. If the new rate is higher or if there's only a small difference in rates, refinancing might not make sense because of the overhead of closing costs. It's worth getting an estimate of closing costs to see how many months of interest savings would be necessary before you come out ahead.

For example, if closing costs are $3,000, but you cut your interest rate on a $240,000 mortgage from 4% to 3%, which saves $200 per month, you'll break even after 15 months, which is probably a great deal if you don't plan to move anytime soon. Just make sure you're comparing closing costs to interest savings, not payment savings. If you have 20 years left on your mortgage and you refinance into a 30-year mortgage, your payments might drop even if your interest rate doesn't, but that won't actually save you any money in the long run.

These efforts take time, but once you cut your interest rate, the savings go on for quite a long time and help you get out of debt faster with no risk. Just make sure 1) you understand when promotional rates expire so you can pay off any refinanced debt before that happens, and 2) you avoid the temptation to take on new debt once you get your rates lowered.

If you don't understand when a promotional rate expires or how rates might change in the future or how you would adjust if rates change, you might be better off not refinancing your debts. Getting into a deal you don't understand is worse than doing nothing.

But if you understand what the terms are and if you can control your spending, there's never any reason to pay more interest than you have to.

Overall, the idea of getting out of debt may seem daunting, and it's not always easy. But the good news is that you can get out of debt with the application of time and self-discipline. As long as you know this is a long-term process and you stick with it, it'll work!

CHAPTER 5:
HOW TO MANAGE CASH

As a kid, I always liked the character of Scrooge McDuck. It looked like a lot of fun to swim in a money bin full of gold coins and bags with dollar signs.

When I suggested to my wife that I wanted to fill our bathtub with gold coins and swim in it, she rolled her eyes at me and made an exasperated sound as if somehow I were wrong. And to give her credit, there may have been a few problems with the idea, notwithstanding that I did have a really great cartoon character to back me up.

For one thing, it probably would hurt to dive headfirst into a pile of metal. For another, it's just a really poor use of capital.

Cash should be in a liquid form. No, that doesn't mean melting the gold coins. Liquid gold is nearly 2,000 degrees, which might damage your bathtub and yourself if you try to swim in it, and you also run the risk of it going down the drain.

While I suppose money down the drain is better than money flushed down the toilet, both are best avoided where liquid gold is concerned.

"Liquid" means easy to access and use as needed. Gold coins have their place, but they can't be used efficiently as money very quickly or easily. Scrooge McDuck messed up on another point: Large amounts of cash don't generate any return on investment, although gold would theoretically keep up with inflation over time.

So what's the best way to manage cash as you accumulate it?

Set up an emergency fund

Emergencies happen. The car is always going to break down at some point. The water heater is going to leak. The roof is going to crack. The toilet is going to clog. The furnace is going to fail. Someone is going to get sick. The cell phone is going to get lost. Your laptop is going to catch on fire after your two-year-old spills motor oil on it and plays with your lighter.

The number of irregular expenses in life is very high, and none of them should ever take you by surprise. The exact timing might be a surprise, and the motor-oil-on-the-laptop is certainly a surprise, but the existence of irregular expenses is one of the certainties in life, just like taxes and extinction-level meteors (or so I've been led to believe based on some movies I watched recently).

Thus, you have a choice of either being prepared or unprepared.

Many people have the plan of "I'll figure it out when it happens." Maybe you'll get lucky, but when your kid hits a baseball through the neighbor's window and smashes a $2,000 Lalique crystal vase, being unprepared means that you either have to borrow at 27.99% on a credit card, or it means you have to tell your neighbor how stupid it is to spend $2,000 on a vase and that you'll never pay for the vase or the window because the whole thing was really his fault for wasting his money in the first place.

Being prepared, on the other hand, would mean that you simply write a check to your neighbor and tell him how stupid he was to spend $2,000 on a vase.

(By the way, this... um... never happened to... me... as a kid).

Obviously, it would be best for your financial future if Rene Lalique had never been born, but the second-best thing is to be prepared.

An emergency fund is simply a source of low-cost capital you can access as needed in order to avoid the need for high-cost capital. The loss of the 0.01% interest from cash in the bank hurts a lot less than the 27.99% interest on your debt. Consuming cash from a bank account to make minimum debt payments hurts a lot less than running up late fees and wrecking your credit. Having money for irregular expenses causes much less debt accumulation than not having money for irregular expenses. And, of course, having a plan for emergencies takes a lot of the stress out of life.

That's really all there is to the theory of an emergency fund: Have money set aside, because you know you'll need it in the future. So how do you set this up?

First, you set a goal. Enough cash to cover 3-6 months of living expenses is probably a good start, both for helping with irregular costs, but also for covering your cash-flow needs in the case of a job loss.

Second, you set aside money. It's not quite as difficult as it looks at first. If you can save 10% of your income, within 2½ years you would have a 3-month emergency fund.

If you can't save 10% of your income, save 5%, or even 1%, and work to increase your savings rate over time. The important thing is that you're starting to build the emergency fund, even if you're starting slowly. Time is your friend if you're moving in the right direction, and you'll get there eventually.

Third, put the cash into an interest-bearing savings account. AllyBank is a good online bank that regularly pays interest in the top tier of most banks, although you can always check Bankrate.com to get current quotes. Unfortunately, interest rates are pretty miserable, and you shouldn't expect that the interest will make a big difference. But, receiving any interest is better receiving no interest.

Back in 2007, it was easy to get 5% on cash, which was quite nice, but I don't believe interest rates, or the South, are going to rise again anytime soon.

That means it's tempting to invest your emergency fund in stocks, for example, where you might get a 7% investment return instead of 1% or less.

However, you're not setting up an emergency fund to generate investment returns; you're setting it up as a *cash and liquidity reserve*. You can't afford to risk your principal on cash you might need at any moment, so the lack of interest doesn't change the calculation.

Don't set up an emergency fund

My wife complains that I'm "contradictory," and this section is no exception. There are times where it makes sense not to have an emergency fund.

Remember that the purpose of an emergency fund is to have access to low-cost capital so that, if you meet with an unexpected financial expense, you can minimize the financial damage to yourself. If you have access to liquid capital at a lower rate than the debts you carry, it makes sense to apply that capital toward your debts.

Our old friend Billy McWasteful has a $15,000 emergency fund in his checking account earning 0% interest. He also has $15,000 in credit-card debt at 27.99%. Effectively, Billy is paying $4,198.50 in annual interest to borrow his own money, which seems rather wasteful to Billy, especially when he'd rather use that money to buy a Lalique crystal vase.

Billy is also a homeowner. He has a home equity line of credit (HELOC) on his house with $50,000 in available credit at 4%.

In that situation, there's no reason for him to have extra cash on hand when it could be applied toward paying off his high-interest credit-card debt. Billy should withdraw all his cash and pay his credit card, thus saving all of the annual interest. If Billy later runs into a financial emergency, he can always borrow on his HELOC at 4% to meet his needs.

Paying 4% would be more expensive than using cash earning 0%, but the money he saves on credit-card interest before he needs the money would more than make up for that.

If Billy were not a homeowner, but if he had a credit card with no balance and a 15% interest rate, he would also be better off taking his cash and paying off his high-interest debt at 27.99%. If Billy needed money later, he could borrow on his 15% credit card to supply his needs.

Obviously borrowing at 15% is undesirable (as is borrowing at all when it can be avoided), and Billy would be well advised to build a cash emergency fund, but that would be something to do only after having paid off his expensive debts to save on interest.

The same principle could be applied if Billy had an investment portfolio with margin credit available at 7%, or any other ready source of capital at an interest rate lower than his most-expensive debt.

Applying your emergency fund cash entirely into debt payment is a more advanced technique for managing your finances. To do this, you have to be comfortable that you have continuous access to capital and that the interest rates won't shift dramatically.

You also have to be confident that you can pay all minimum payments on all your debts in the event of a job loss or other catastrophe (e.g., that your credit card won't stop working and you won't hit your credit limit if you have no income for an extended period).

If you're not sure on either point, then it's better to keep things simple and understandable by having emergency cash on hand, even if you're not minimizing your interest expense.

Beyond the emergency fund

Once you've reached your goal of building your emergency fund, you can move additional cash into other priorities. "Fully funded" is a somewhat subjective term that depends on your risk tolerance.

If you're a risk taker who wants to move your finances along more quickly, a three-month emergency fund is probably enough. If you want to operate more conservatively and slowly, a six-month emergency fund is fine. However, there is a limit. An emergency fund that covers more than six months' worth of expenses actually starts to hurt you.

Although cash on hand provides a feeling of security, cash produces very little or no return on investment, and it decays over time with the effect of inflation. Additional cash beyond what you need for emergencies should be applied first toward debt reduction, and second toward investments. If you want to set aside cash for other near-term needs, such as a major purchase or a home down payment, there's nothing wrong with that, but eventually you have to invest your cash in order to create long-term wealth.

CHAPTER 6:
UNDERSTANDING INVESTMENT ACCOUNTS

Long ago, in the ancient history of America, if you wanted to make an investment you would simply take your money and buy something. There were no acronyms or special rules to consider. You didn't need any special accounts. There wasn't even an income tax. All you had to do was make your best investment decision and focus on the future.

Long ago, you also would die at 40 if you got a splinter or had an infected tooth, and the best doctors were the ones who knew what kind of liquor to give you before they amputated your leg because of the infection they caused by not washing their tools before doing surgery. Stock trading was slow and expensive, and information was scarce.

There weren't even indoor toilets, so for people who were wasting money at the time, I have no idea what they flushed it down.

I'm under no impression that the ancient past was ideal or automatically better than things are now, but in the sense that the tax code was easier to understand and you didn't have to make investment decisions in the context of tax efficiency, things were simpler.

We now have a beneficent tax code that creates a whole menagerie of investment-account types, all with different rules, tax consequences, and optimization strategies. You still have to make good investment decisions, but now you also have to make good account-type decisions to avoid some of your hard work leaking out in the form of extra taxes.

If you make investments without understanding the tax consequences of the account type you're using, the government will happily correct the error by taking a larger percentage of your money. Nobody will tell you that you're making a mistake or that you could save money by using a different type of account. The only defense against this kind of loss is to know what you're doing.

The good news is that this field is not difficult to navigate. There are only two basic categories of accounts: taxable and retirement. Within the retirement category, there are many subtypes, but most people use only two or three types at most. You also don't have to worry too much about the details. Once you understand the basic idea of what the account is supposed to do, you can look up the details later.

Taxable accounts

A taxable account is the simplest account to understand. You can deposit whatever amount of money you want into it, and you may take your money out at any time. There are no rules or penalties or deductions to worry about.

So why not stop there and make all your investments in a taxable account? Because it's taxable, of course. If you receive a dividend, that's taxed. If you generate a capital gain, that's taxed too. If you receive interest, there's a tax. Of course, if you're receiving interest, chances are you're living in an alternate universe where interest rates are over 0%, and while I can't provide much useful advice about alternate universes, I can say I've never read anything positive about them (although if my book is available in an alternate universe, then kudos to the publisher).

But in this world, taxable accounts serve a useful purpose as a place to hold investments where you want maximum flexibility to move money in and out, even if you have to pay taxes from time to time. They're an essential component of your investing toolkit, especially if early retirement is a goal for you.

Taxable accounts are distinct from retirement accounts, a much broader category with many more rules, but if you understand those rules, you'll be able to control your tax bill to some extent, and considering that taxes are often one of the largest expenses in a personal budget, this is exceptionally important for long-term wealth creation.

Retirement accounts break down into three basic categories: Traditional, Roth, and Health Savings Account. The latter, of course, has additional medical-expense elements to it, but it's useful to think of it in retirement-account terms.

Traditional retirement accounts

Traditional retirement accounts help you to save on your income tax when you contribute money. There are no taxes on investment income within the retirement account, and the lack of taxes should help the account to grow faster than it would in a taxable account. However, the government still wants its money, much the same way that a ravenous tiger would want the hamburger you promised it if you made it wait twenty years, and when you withdraw money from a traditional retirement account, the government assesses income taxes on the withdrawal.

The ideal method for using a traditional retirement account is to make contributions while you're working and in a high tax bracket, thus saving income taxes now, and upon retirement, presumably when your income is lower and you're in a lower tax bracket, you make withdrawals and pay your tax.

For example, if you're working and paying taxes at 30%, contributing to a traditional retirement account and saving 30% in taxes now is much more valuable than the expense you'll incur in your retired future when you owe 15% on the withdrawals. You can double up on this with state taxes. Most states allow deductions for retirement contributions, and if you save state income tax during your career and then move to a state with no income tax in retirement, that money is permanently saved.

Of course, there's an element of guesswork in this. Although you know your tax rate now, there's no way to know your future tax rate or how much income you'll have. There's also no way to know in advance if your fickle spouse is suddenly going to develop a love of cave diving that forces you to move to a state with high income taxes. However, if you believe your current tax rate is high, either because your income is very high or you live in a high-tax state, and if you don't think you'll have to move to a high-tax state for cave diving, then the odds are probably in your favor that your tax rate may be lower in retirement than it is now.

With the benefit of being able to shift your taxes into the future comes a big limitation. Except for a few limited cases, if you withdraw money from a traditional retirement account before age 59 ½ (I have no idea why it's 59 ½ instead of 59 or 60), the government charges you a 10% penalty tax on top of income taxes on that withdrawal. This is intended to incentivize you to leave your money alone for retirement, which you should be doing anyway.

Since this penalty means traditional retirement accounts should be left alone until retirement, make sure you have an emergency fund set up first before you begin locking away money for the future. After all, the easiest way to avoid the 10% early-withdrawal penalty is by not making early withdrawals. The second-easiest way to avoid the penalty is dying, which I generally don't recommend as a financial-planning tool.

Traditional retirement accounts also come with another special feature: Required Minimum Distributions (RMD). The government won't wait forever to get its money. If you're age 72 or older, the IRS has a special formula to calculate how much money you have to take out of your account and how much of it they get.

The withdrawal amount generally increases with age and based on your life expectancy, so when you're 72, you'll have to withdraw about 4% of your account, at age 80 you'll have to withdraw about 5%, at age 90 you'll have to withdraw 9%, and so forth.

The really neat thing here is that the IRS is very optimistic about potential lifespans. The RMD table goes all the way up to age 115, at which point you'll have to withdraw 50% of your IRA balance each year. If you make it to age 120, the withdrawal rate won't increase, but if you're pulling out 50% of your IRA balance each year and paying taxes on it, chances are there won't be much left to withdraw. Even if there were still a large IRA balance, at age 120 you could die at any second, and tax planning probably isn't going to be a major concern at that point in your life.

Instead, it's far more useful to look at the traditional-retirement account landscape and all the varieties it contains. Despite the variety, these accounts all function in basically the same way.

Traditional IRA. This is an account you can open on your own at any bank or brokerage company. The annual contribution limit is $6,000 (or $7,000 if you're age 50 or over). If you're not covered by a workplace retirement plan, you can deduct your contributions regardless of your income.

If you are covered by a retirement plan at work, then you might not be permitted to deduct contributions if your income is over $66,000 for a single filer or $105,000 for a married couple. In that case, and without a deduction, there's really no point to putting money in a traditional IRA, although you are allowed to do that in something called a non-deductible IRA.

You may open a traditional IRA for each of you and your spouse. Even if your spouse is working as a homemaker, which the IRS doesn't consider to be work because you're not getting paid for it, you're permitted to contribute up to $6,000 to your spouse's traditional IRA, which effectively doubles the contribution.

Traditional IRAs allow you to invest in just about anything you want. The investment flexibility in these is second only to the flexibility of a taxable account or a bendy straw (which I know from personal experience to be both a very flexible object and also a very poor investment).

<u>401(k)</u>. This is an extremely common type of retirement plan. This requires an employer sponsor, and if your employer offers it, there are no income limits for deducting contributions. You could make $10 million per year and still make tax-deductible contributions. Contributions typically come out of your paycheck, so you get the benefit of reduced taxes immediately, as well as the convenience of not having to think about contributing.

The annual contribution limit is $19,500, although some employers may impose their own limits. If you're over age 50, the contribution limit is $26,000. Each spouse may have a separate 401(k) account, so the limit is effectively doubled for married couples.

One great feature of 401(k) plans is that many employers will offer matching contributions. For example, if your employer offers a 50% match and you contribute $5,000, your employer will contribute an additional $2,500 for you, and there are no taxes due on that match until you make withdrawals in the future. Even better, employer contributions are never subject to Social Security or Medicare taxes.

Matching contributions are at the discretion of your employer, but if it is offered, you should contribute enough money to collect the full match. After all, your employer is offering you extra money for free, and all you have to do to receive it is save for your future, which you should be doing anyway.

Most 401(k) plans limit you to mutual funds or other investments chosen by your employer. Investment flexibility varies dramatically from plan to plan, but low-cost index funds are usually available and make for a good choice if you don't have anything you like better.

403(b). This is the same type of account as a 401(k), but it's for government and non-profit plans. Many 403(b) plans come with additional management fees that are less common in 401(k) plans. Some plans, for example, charge high annual fees or high surrender fees if you exit the plan within a certain number of years. If your employer offers a 403(b) plan, it might make sense to contribute, but you need to read the details of the fees very carefully first.

SEP-IRA. This type of plan is less common, except with small employers. Typically, the employer makes a contribution on your behalf based on your earnings at the company. You don't get any say in how much money is deposited, but it's a great benefit if you are covered by one of these.

If you're self-employed, you may create a SEP-IRA on your own and contribute up to 20% of your net, self-employment income. The contribution limit is $58,000 based on your first $290,000 of income. This is the highest contribution limit of any typical retirement plan, and even if you make more than $290,000, you can still contribute, subject to the $58,000 cap.

457. This type of plan is found almost exclusively in the government

and non-profit area. It's more common than unicorns, but less common than leprechauns. The contribution limits are generally the same as for 401(k) and 403(b) plans, but there's considerable variation from company to company.

Some plans are 457(b) varieties which are very similar to 403(b) plans, but with some additional options for contributing more money or taking withdrawals without penalty. Some plans are 457(f) varieties aimed at highly-compensated employees, which allow nearly unlimited contributions, but which require taking a distribution and paying taxes on the entire balance upon separation from service, which could result in a massive tax bill and is the complete opposite of what you'd want a retirement plan to do for you.

Since the variety of terms in 457 plans are so broad, it's wise to approach these cautiously before contributing. But since you'll probably never see a 457 plan, at least that's one less thing to think about.

Roth retirement accounts

Roth retirement accounts are basically the opposite of traditional retirement accounts: You pay all of your taxes upfront, but withdrawals in the future are tax free.

Like the traditional retirement accounts, no taxes are due on income generated within the account.

Roth accounts are ideal for people who are in low tax brackets, for example people who are just starting their careers and aren't earning much, people who have lots of tax credits and minimal tax liabilities (e.g., someone with five kids getting five child tax credits), or people who earn less in a given year than they expect to make in future years (e.g., you receive lower sales commissions or no bonus).

The bet you're making is that the tax rate you're paying now is less than the tax rate you'll be paying in the future. You're also making a bet that Congress won't change the rules on taxing Roth accounts in the future.

One of the neat features of personal finance, investing, and tax planning is that there's an element of guessing involved. Nobody knows what future tax rates are going to be or what your income situation will look like. And that's one of the reasons why you don't have to worry about being an expert in finance in order to manage your finances: There is no expert anywhere in the world who knows the future any better than you do.

Thus, Roth accounts are a great way to create a pool of potentially tax-free money for yourself in the future. That gives you flexibility, even if you don't know what to expect.

The limits for Roth contributions generally mirror those of Traditional retirement accounts, but the withdrawal rules are a bit different.

If you've owned any Roth account for at least five years, you may withdraw your contributions at any time with no tax and no penalties. After all, you already paid taxes on the income you contributed, and it wouldn't make sense to tax your money twice. That feature alone makes the accounts quite useful as a low-cost source of capital at any age, although you want to limit Roth withdrawals when possible. Once you take the money out, you can't contribute it back again.

Earnings (e.g., dividends and capital gains), on the other hand, are a different matter. If you withdraw those before age 59 ½, they are subject to income taxes and a 10% penalty, so withdrawing those early is a really bad idea. After age 59 ½, there are no taxes on any Roth withdrawals.

Since there are no taxes on withdrawals taken later in life, the government doesn't care if you leave the money in the account or if you take it out. Thus, there are no required minimum distributions. You can leave all your Roth money invested until you're 115 and not pay any taxes on anything in the account. The big challenge in that case is living to age 115.

Within the Roth universe, there are two basic account types.

<u>Roth IRA</u>. This is an account you can open on your own at any bank or brokerage company. The annual contribution limit is $6,000 (or $7,000 if you're age 50 or over), the same as with a traditional IRA. Having a workplace retirement plan doesn't affect your eligibility to contribute to a Roth IRA.

Contributions are, however, limited by your income. If your income is over $139,000 for a single person or $206,000 for a married couple, you might not be eligible to contribute. However, if your income is over those limits, you're not going to be in the lowest tax brackets, in which case one of the traditional retirement plans might make more sense.

As with the traditional IRA, you may open a Roth IRA for each of you and your spouse. Even if your spouse is not working, you're permitted to contribute up to $6,000 to your spouse's Roth IRA, which effectively doubles the contribution.

Roth IRAs allow you to invest in just about anything you want. The investment flexibility in these is second only to the flexibility of a taxable account.

<u>Roth 401(k) and Roth 403(b)</u>. These are uncommon plan types. They mirror the traditional 401(k) and the traditional 403(b) plans in most respects, except that as Roth plans they are funded with after-tax dollars, and withdrawals come out tax-free in retirement.

The annual contribution limit is $19,500, although some employers may impose their own limits. If you're over age 50, the contribution limit is $26,000.

Most Roth 401(k) and 403(b) plans limit you to mutual funds or other investments chosen by your employer. Investment flexibility varies dramatically from plan to plan, but very commonly low-cost index funds are available.

If your employer matches 401(k) contributions, they typically match Roth 401(k) contributions as well. However, because the employer match would not be tax-free within the Roth account, the employer has to place the match into a traditional 401(k) account instead in order to avoid an immediate tax liability.

This administrative headache is the reason most employers don't offer these plans. But if such a plan is offered to you, it's always great to have the option.

Health savings accounts

Health savings accounts (HSA) are probably the most tax-advantaged accounts in existence. Contributions get you an immediate tax deduction, and many withdrawals can come out tax free. I'm not the kind of person to use the phrase "the cat's pajamas," but if I were, this account would be it.

Here's how they work: Each year, you can contribute up to $3,600 if you're single, and $7,200 if you're married or have kids. Individuals age 55 or older may contribute an additional $1,000 each year.

If you open and fund the account on your own, you get a tax deduction for your contribution, saving you income tax and state income tax. If the account is opened and funded through your employer, contributions also lower your Social Security and Medicare tax, a benefit not available to traditional IRA and 401(k) contributions.

Most health savings account plans offer a variety of mutual fund investment options, although some allow for you to invest in anything you want. The exact choices depend on the particular plan. Investment income within the account is tax free.

Now for the really great part: Withdrawals (both contributions and earnings) taken for qualified medical expenses are tax free, regardless of your age.

The term "qualified medical expenses" is extremely broad. It includes doctor visits, hospitalization, prescriptions, dental expenses, orthodontia, glasses, contacts, co-pays, deductibles, medical devices, hearing aids, guide dogs, and many other things not typically covered by insurance. It also covers the cost of travel to and from the medical facility at which services are provided, at least within reason. If you decide to have an annual physical with your "regular" doctor in Tahiti and you fly there by private jet, the IRS might question if the expense was medically necessary, but if you need to travel to another state to see a specialist for a rare disease, you'll have no issue.

If you withdraw money for non-medical expenses, however, you will have to pay ordinary income tax on the withdrawal, plus a 20% penalty. Don't do that.

Oddly enough, over-the-counter medications, such as Tylenol and Claritin, are not considered "medical expenses" by the IRS. Perhaps people like running around taking allergy medicine for entertainment. Using HSA funds to pay for over-the-counter medicine subjects the distribution to income taxes and the 20% penalty. This rule was enacted with the passage of Obamacare, which also increased the withdrawal penalty from 10% to 20%, and it's puzzling to speculate how this was supposed to make medical care more affordable, but such are the current laws.

You don't have to worry about contributing too much to the account and getting stuck with money you can't use if you're healthy. Any money that's left over accumulates over time and may be invested. By the time you reach age 65, you get an additional option: You may withdraw money for any purpose at all without a penalty (although you'll still owe ordinary income tax). Medical expense withdrawals remain, of course, tax free. At that age, effectively your HSA becomes a traditional IRA with a bonus tax-free withdrawal option for medical expenses. As I said, the cat's pajamas.

All in all, you'll never find another account with as many tax benefits as the health savings account.

Unfortunately, unlike an IRA or other retirement plan, not everyone is eligible to contribute to an HSA. Contributions are allowed only for people who are: over 18, covered by a high-deductible health plan, not a dependent, and not enrolled in Medicare. Limiting access to these wonderful accounts does nothing to make medicine more affordable, but that's what it is.

"High deductible health plans" need to carry a minimum annual deductible of $1,400 for individuals and $2,800 for families, and a maximum out-of-pocket cost of $7,000 for individuals and $14,000 for families. There are other plan requirements as well, but eligible plans are generally marketed as "HSA compatible."

Rollovers

As annoying as the investment-account laws are, they at least provide flexibility on rollovers, which simply means moving money from one account to another.

For taxable accounts, you have the freedom to move or combine your taxable accounts in any way you like without tax or penalty.

For retirement accounts, you can generally move like accounts into or out of one another. That is to say, you can move one type of traditional retirement account into another type of traditional retirement account, or one type of Roth account into another type of Roth account, all without tax or penalty.

For example, if you have a traditional 401(k) from an old employer, you can roll over the balance from that plan into your traditional IRA or into a 401(k) with a new employer. If you have a Roth 403(b), you can roll over that balance into your Roth IRA. One HSA can be rolled over into another HSA.

Some individual plans have specific rules or fees, but the government at least won't get in your way.

The rollovers themselves can be done in two different ways.

The most common type is a "trustee-to-trustee" or "direct" rollover. This happens when you ask one account custodian, for example, your old employer who holds your old 401(k) plan, to send the money directly to your traditional IRA held by your brokerage company.

For example, if you have $50,000 in the 401(k) at your old employer, you can call them and have them send the money directly to your traditional IRA. You never touch the money, you don't owe any taxes, and you don't even have to report anything on your income tax. Easy.

The "60-day rollover" or "indirect rollover" is similar, except that the old trustee would send you a check for the balance in your old 401(k), and it would be up to you to deposit the money into your traditional IRA within 60 days.

You almost never want to do an indirect rollover. If you do that, the previous trustee generally must withhold income taxes from the check you receive, but you're still responsible for depositing the full balance into your other IRA. For example, if you're moving $50,000 from an old 401(k) to your traditional IRA, your 401(k) provider would send you a check for only $40,000, and it would be your problem to deposit the full $50,000 into your traditional IRA within 60 days. The missing $10,000 goes directly to the IRS.

When you file your tax return the next year, you have to report the distribution and the rollover, and you'll receive a refund of the $10,000 withholding. You get the money back, but it's not terribly convenient being out $10,000 until tax time. Worse yet, if you're not able to get the full $50,000 into your IRA within 60 days, you become liable for income taxes and penalties on the distribution.

Save yourself the trouble and just do direct rollovers.

But make the rollovers! It's important that your investments should be easy to manage. If you have a traditional IRA and five different 401(k) plans from different employers, you'll have a hard time keeping track of what you're investing in and what your fees are.

If you roll over the balances from your old 401(k) plans and put them all in your traditional IRA, then everything is in one place which makes life much easier.

Roth conversions

To add to the complexity, traditional IRAs can be converted into Roth IRAs. For example, if you have $100,000 in your traditional IRA (perhaps from rolled-over 401(k) contributions), you might decide that you want distributions in the future to be tax free, and you'd prefer for this balance to become a Roth IRA.

After you tell your broker you want to convert your account, the $100,000 gets added to your Roth IRA balance, and the IRS adds $100,000 to your taxable income. You then have to pay the tax on this additional "income" when you file your tax return the next year.

The upside is that you never have to pay taxes on anything coming out of this account for the rest of your life. The downside is that you have to pay taxes now. There are two ways to pay the conversion tax: You can pay it out of your traditional IRA balance, or you can pay it with cash you already have in a taxable account.

If you pay the tax out of your traditional IRA balance, you'll owe income taxes for the money you took out to pay the income taxes, and if you're under 59 ½, you'll also owe a 10% penalty. Ah, there's nothing as much fun as paying taxes on your taxes.

If you pay the tax out of cash on hand, then at least there's no additional tax or penalty.

Roth IRA conversions make sense under many circumstances. For example, if you have a year with abnormally-low income, then you might not mind converting some of your traditional IRA balance to a Roth IRA while you're still in a low tax bracket. Or if you're planning to move from a low-tax state to a high-tax state, you might want to make the conversion to avoid state taxes on future IRA withdrawals.

However, you should almost never convert a traditional IRA to a Roth IRA if you don't have enough cash on hand to pay the tax on the conversion. And there's almost never a reason to do a Roth IRA conversion if you're in a high-tax state or a high tax bracket.

Which is better: the Roth IRA or the traditional IRA?

The Roth IRA vs. traditional IRA debate is the second-biggest question in the life of people who are eligible to contribute to both types of accounts (the biggest question is whether my wife thinks I'm wrong about everything, or just wrong about most things).

It reminds me of the story of the man who goes to his doctor, and he says, "Doctor, my brother thinks he's a chicken. What should I do?" The doctor asks, "have you considered taking your brother to a psychiatrist?" The man responds, "Yes, but I need the eggs."

You may not need either a psychiatrist or eggs, but you're right if you guessed that there's no mathematical answer to the Roth IRA vs. Traditional IRA question, unless you know what future tax rates are going to be and how much money you're going to earn. However, I believe Roth IRAs are probably better for most people in most circumstances.

Traditional IRAs generate great tax savings up front, but those tax savings don't help you in the long run unless you invest them for the future. Most people spend whatever they save in taxes, and anything that encourages you to spend more is going to make it harder to reach your financial goals.

The second point in favor of the Roth is the higher effective contribution limit. If you can protect from taxes $6,000 in a traditional IRA or $6,000 in a Roth IRA, the latter is far more valuable. That's for the simple reason that the traditional IRA carries with it a built-in tax liability for when you make withdrawals in the future, whereas the Roth IRA has no such liability.

Let's say taxes are 30%. If you contribute $6,000 in a traditional IRA and then withdraw it in retirement, you'll have $4,200. If you contribute $6,000 to a Roth IRA and withdraw it in retirement, you'll have $6,000.

While the traditional IRA gets you an immediate tax deduction, if you can afford to skip the tax deduction, the Roth IRA lets you shelter $6,000 in tax-free growth instead of $4,200.

Other times the traditional IRA is more valuable. If you have high income, the tax deduction from a traditional IRA is more valuable. And if your income is very high, you're probably not eligible for a Roth IRA contribution anyway, which makes the point moot.

If you're in a high-tax state like California, the traditional IRA deduction could save you 10% upfront, and if you retire in a state like Florida with 0% income tax, you effectively get a tax-free Roth conversion in the process, which is really hard to beat!

The other point in favor of traditional IRAs is that you can limit your risk for future Congressional shenanigans. The Roth IRA is supposed to be tax free forever, but it's not hard to imagine a scenario in which a money-hungry Congress deplores people "not paying their fair share" by hiding money, untaxed, in Roth IRAs and changes the rules to make distributions taxable. By having money in a traditional IRA, you make yourself less at risk. Of course, it's also possible the Roth IRA rules won't change.

Since we don't know what the rules are going to be in the future, and since we don't know what tax rates are going to be, and since most workplace retirement plans are of the traditional variety, contributions you make on your own should be made to Roth accounts for tax diversification. Then, no matter what the tax situation is in the future, you have different resources you can draw upon depending on what makes the most sense at the time.

More important than which accounts you use, though, is that you should save and invest as much as you can. Saving a large amount of money in the wrong account will help you far more than saving a small amount of money in the right account.

CHAPTER 7:
UNDERSTANDING INVESTMENTS

One of the fundamental principles of investing is that you should invest only in things you understand.

A few years ago, when Bitcoin seemed to be doubling in value almost weekly, I heard one cashier at a fast-food restaurant telling another cashier about how much money he was making on his Bitcoin investments. At the same time, another person I knew quit his job to become a Bitcoin broker, another person borrowed $10,000 on his credit card to buy Bitcoin, and a third person borrowed most of his home equity to buy Bitcoin.

It's possible that these people understood the fundamental principles behind blockchain technologies and potential shifts in supply and demand for Bitcoin that would validate their investments as profitable in the long run, but I suspect they understood only that the price was going up a lot, and they wanted to make money quickly like everyone else.

I don't know how things turned out for the cashier. After I received my sandwich, I could have asked him for his contact information so I could monitor his inevitable downfall, but I have sense enough to know that you should always be nice to the people who handle your food when you're not looking. I also really enjoyed my sandwich. But I do know that the guy who became a Bitcoin broker was never heard from again, the guy who borrowed on his credit card (which amounted to 25% of his annual salary) struggled under the debt, and the person who borrowed his home equity ended up in foreclosure.

These people all made multiple, major errors in their investments. Two of those errors were using too much debt and failing to diversify. Ironically, Bitcoin ended up rising significantly several years later, and excessive debt and short-term thinking made it impossible for them to benefit from this. But the most significant error was simply not understanding Bitcoin, its risks, and the rationale for why it would be a good investment.

Instead of using judgment about whether or not Bitcoin made sense as an investment at a given price, these individuals saw the price rising and simply assumed the price would continue rising forever, thus justifying borrowing money and going all-in on the bet.

It seems silly, but people look at short-term price movements all the time and assume those trends shall continue forever. During the housing bubble, people took out excessive loans and banks lent money recklessly all on the premise that the price of real estate prices would increase rapidly forever (they didn't).

During the Dot-Com bubble, people saw money-losing internet companies going up in value for years, and they invested heavily expecting that prices would continue rising forever (they didn't).

Whenever the stock market drops significantly, people panic and sell their investments when prices are at their lowest, fearful that prices shall continue dropping forever (they don't).

When people have steady employment income, they borrow money to spend on stuff now, assuming they can always pay it back later from future paychecks at a job that will never end (eventually every job ends from a retirement, layoff, death, disability, etc.).

Outside of the financial world, you might look at fashion and assume that, because men have had to wear neckties since the 1870's, men will continue to have to wear neckties forever. Unlike some of the other examples above, this assumption about the future is probably correct; women's fashions change almost daily, but men's fashions, at least more formal fashions, generally lack creativity and change only once every 100 – 200 years.

Looking at anything in motion and extrapolating that motion into the future is a basic human instinct, and for the most part, it's actually quite useful. That instinct is precisely what allows you to drive safely and to predict where other cars are going to be when you change lanes. It's the same thing that allows sports players to be able to run and catch a ball.

[Incidentally, I hate sports. The utter pointlessness of chasing a ball from one place to another and the amount of time and money that goes into the sports industry seems like a tragic waste. I'd rather see the government dump 500,000 tons of concrete into the ocean than build a sports stadium; the concrete would also be a waste, but at least it would be cheaper. I'll only grudgingly accept the occasional sports metaphor if it has practicality in conveying ideas, but not if I can find a non-sport metaphor. Although I do like bowling.]

Once you realize most people assume that whatever is happening now will continue into the future forever, you can make a conscious decision to avoid that trap for yourself. Never make an investment decision simply because the price of something is going up or down. You must understand why the price is moving up or down and then make a judgment about whether a reasonable price is higher or lower.

More broadly, if you don't understand what the thing is that people are buying and selling, it's best not to get involved.

Fortunately, most investments fall into only a small number of basic categories and are not difficult to understand.

Bank accounts

Bank accounts almost aren't even worth counting as investments now that interest no longer exists, but they still are quite useful. They come in three basic varieties: checking accounts, savings or money-market accounts, and certificates of deposit (CDs).

The basic checking account is a place where you make deposits and pay bills. Some banks charge monthly fees for the privilege of letting you access your own money, but it's not difficult to find a bank offering a checking account with no fees or with easy-to-meet requirements for waiving fees. Even though almost nobody uses a check anymore, everyone needs a checking account as a central place for managing your income and payments.

Savings, or money-market accounts, which are basically the same thing, are designed as places where you can put money you're not expecting to move very often. Some banks impose a limit on the number of withdrawals per month out of a savings account. The reason for that is partly to encourage you to leave the money in place, but mostly because of obsolete banking regulations.

Savings accounts used to compensate people for this inconvenience by paying interest, but realistically, interest is something of a joke these days. It's not even a funny joke. It's more like a joke about a disabled kid which is both in poor taste and lacking a punchline.

A little interest is better than no interest at all, especially as your cash balances grow over time, but you don't have to spend much time thinking about interest rates on savings. I, for one, would rather spend time thinking about sports, which I hate, than about the paltry interest currently offered.

CDs are ultra-inconvenient savings accounts. You lock away your money for some period of time, and, in exchange, you get a higher rate of interest than a savings account would pay. If you want your money before the end of the time period, you might have to pay a penalty.

Once upon a time, CDs had a useful purpose, but why would you want to lock up your money for any period of time in exchange for a slightly larger amount of interest when interest is nothing? There's really no reason to bother with CDs anymore, but if you have a very large amount of cash that you want to hang on to in a CD, a minimal interest rate at least means that the penalty is also minimal since it's usually defined as a certain number of months of interest.

Despite their lack of exciting features and the very poor returns, bank accounts are incredibly useful as parking places for emergency funds. That's for the simple reason that you can't afford to take any risk with money you might need at any moment. Imagine the horror of losing your job during an economic downturn, only to see that your emergency fund was invested in something that also collapsed during the downturn.

Cash accounts in banks never lose money. Even if the bank goes out of business, government FDIC insurance covers the loss; you know your money shall always be there when you need it.

Similarly, if you expect to need money within the next 3-5 years, you should keep that money in a bank account. For example, if you're saving for a down payment on a house that you plan to buy in the next few years, you don't want to take an investment loss right before you're about to buy.

With this safety and with this guarantee of never losing money, you do pay a price, and that price is that you'll never make money either.

Sure, you might get 1% in some savings accounts, or even 1.5% in some bank CDs, but the interest generated is almost always going to be less than inflation, and you'll almost always lose real value over time.

That's why bank accounts are sort of like carrots. There might be a usefulness in eating a few of them, but if you eat exclusively carrots, you're going to be a miserable person who hates the world and who is hated in return. Once your emergency fund is filled and your short-term savings goals are funded, you can reasonably say you have enough cash. Any additional money you save should be invested elsewhere so that it can start helping you instead of dragging you down.

Bonds

Bonds are much like bank CDs; they have a fixed value and pay out interest until some maturity date when they get cashed in. But unlike bank CDs, they don't come with FDIC insurance. If the bond issuer goes out of business, there's no guarantee you'll get your money back (although usually you get back some or all of your money).

Worse yet, bonds are often illiquid; you might not be able to sell them if you need the money right away, or if you are able to sell them, you might not get back the full face value. Although bonds have a fixed value just like a bank CD, the value of a bond before the maturity date can go up and down based on interest rates and the perceived creditworthiness of the issuer.

For this inconvenience and risk, bond issuers traditionally have had to pay more interest than bank accounts. And they still often pay out more interest than banks do, but not enough to make bonds worth the inconvenience.

For example, there are some 100-year bonds issued by universities that pay out 3% per year. Is 3% per year enough interest to make it worth waiting 100 years to get your money back, assuming the university is even around in 100 years to pay you back? Probably not.

There are some government bonds in Europe and Japan that actually have negative interest rates. That means you have to pay the government for the privilege of letting the government use your money and giving less money back to you at a later date. There's no reason ever to take that deal as compared to putting cash in the bank.

Some organizations have a use for low-interest bonds. Apple, for example, can't put $100 billion in the bank without causing major problems, so they might buy government bonds paying nothing. But for most individuals, bonds no longer serve any purpose. Sort of like the appendix, they have outlived their usefulness. To the extent you want a non-volatile asset to mitigate investment volatility, the flexibility of cash is far superior to the extra, tiny, itsy-bitsy interest from bonds.

Stocks

Amusement parks have many types of rides, from merry-go-rounds to roller coasters.

Roller coasters are objectively more fun than merry-go-rounds. There's a chance that a roller coaster might suffer a mechanical breakdown and decapitate all of the riders, but if you look at their operating history over a long period of time, the actual number of decapitations is quite small. On the whole, roller-coaster riders enjoy their amusement-park experience more than the merry-go-round riders.

Part of it is that the riders on the roller coaster get to have more fun, and the other part is that the person riding the merry-go-round almost always ends up having to hold the bags for all the people on the fun rides. Sometimes the merry-go-round rider also has to buy the horribly-overpriced amusement-park food, and having had the experience of buying $7.00 hot dogs and $6.00 sodas for my kids, I can tell you that the merry-go-round is a whole lot less fun than the roller coaster.

Investment options are similar. Stocks are like the roller coaster, and while bank accounts aren't exactly merry-go-rounds, they're more like the bench for the person who isn't riding or having any fun at all.

A stock is simply a small ownership interest in a company. If the Anime Figurine Company is split up into 1 million shares, and you buy 100 shares, you own 0.01% of the whole company.

Stock owners can make money in two main ways: dividends and capital gains. A dividend is your share of the profits the company distributes. If the Anime Figurine Company earns $10 million and distributes all of it as a dividend, then you would receive $10 for every share you own, or $1,000.

A capital gain is the profit you make when you sell your shares for more than you paid. If you purchased your 100 shares of the Anime Figurine Company at $75 each, and you sell them for $125, you make a profit of $50 per share, or $5,000 total.

Over long periods of time, the combination of dividends and capital gains drives your investment returns and leads to massive wealth creation.

Stocks, of course, are not guaranteed. They don't come with any insurance, and it's possible to lose money. In fact, it's almost certain that you'll lose money from time to time. But like the roller coaster, the vast majority of stock investors have a successful adventure without any major problems, and even fewer stock investors get decapitated.

Because many people are scared of stocks or don't understand them, it creates an opportunity to benefit from a return on investment that's far higher than on bonds or cash. It's not unreasonable to expect to double your money every ten years or so without taking excessive risk.

Over shorter periods of time, though, anything can happen, and the shorter the time period, the more unpredictable. If you can invest for 100 years, you're virtually guaranteed to get a good return. If you invest for fifty years or thirty years, you'll do great. Even ten-year investments do well typically.

Five-year periods almost always do well, but there is some risk of a loss. Within one year, you'll make money more often than you lose, but you will lose a lot, and from day to day, winning or losing is just flipping a coin.

Thus, stock investments are best suited for long-term time horizons, meaning a minimum of five years, and preferably at least ten.

Mutual funds

Many people are intimidated by the idea of investing their own money. The investment industry prides itself on creating unnecessary acronyms and jargon designed to confuse people, while also laying out complex investment plans that are difficult for the average person to follow.

This is done for two purposes. The first is to make you think that you don't know what you're doing. If you feel intimidated and lack confidence in yourself, you're more likely to pay an investment company to understand everything for you. The second is to make you think the investment company is really sophisticated and knows what it's doing, which also makes you more inclined to pay them. The investment companies puff up themselves and put you down, and it works.

The reality is much simpler. Investing is just a function of guessing the future. You can make educated guesses based on historic patterns and you can make really complicated models to show how smart you are, but even the smartest investment expert can't tell you what's going to happen tomorrow.

Was there anyone who successfully predicted the September 11th terrorist attacks on September 10th? Did anyone know in advance about Coronavirus? Could anyone in 2006, when Nokia flip phones reigned supreme, have guessed that Apple would invent the iPhone in 2007? More significant, did any investment model predict that Popeye's would eventually develop a really great chicken sandwich?

Of course not!

Nobody knows the future, no matter how fancy his investment theories. And that's an advantage you have: You know as much about the future as everybody else.

Still, mutual funds have uses from time to time, so it's important to understand what mutual funds are: a common pool of capital with an investment manager who picks out stocks and bonds.

They work very similarly to stocks. They are not guaranteed, they can go up and down in value, they are best as long-term investments, and you you're your money from dividends and capital gains.

Unlike stocks, however, you have to pay the mutual fund a management fee for picking out investments for you. The fee is usually deducted from the fund directly, so you rarely see it. That's for convenience, but it also makes it easier for the fund and the fund manager to charge you high fees if you don't get a monthly bill in the mail.

So why would you want to use a mutual fund rather than picking out your own stocks? Sometimes you don't have a choice. Some 401(k) and other retirement plans have only mutual fund choices. Other people pick mutual funds because they're not sure what they're doing, and they feel more confident having someone else picking investments for them. Some people who are starting out might buy mutual funds so they can easily get a more diversified portfolio with many different investments right from the beginning.

There's nothing wrong with any of those reasons, and it's better to pay a mutual fund fee than it is not to invest at all.

Interestingly, there's one simple metric that is very predictive about which mutual funds are likely to perform the best: fees. The funds that have the highest fees typically perform worse than the ones that have the lowest fees.

It makes sense. All the investments in the world generate an average return. That's the definition of average. If you divide up all of those average returns into random pools, the random pools are going to be average too. But when you start deducting management fees out of each pool, the pool that has a bigger fee deducted from its average performance will do worse than the pool that has a smaller fee deducted from its average performance.

So, if you find yourself in a position of wanting or having to pick a mutual fund investment, choose the one with the lowest fees.

Exchange traded funds (ETFs)

Exchange traded funds (ETFs) work just like mutual funds, but they typically own a pre-defined basket of stocks or bonds. For example, some ETFs own all the stocks in the S&P 500 index. Since the basket of stocks doesn't require any judgment or fancy modeling, the management fees are usually extremely small.

ETFs thus will typically perform better than mutual funds, but there are exceptions. For example, some mutual funds use the same kind of passive-investing strategy, such as buying every stock in the S&P 500 index, and charge low fees. And some ETFs are fairly esoteric or complex, and have higher fees.

But by and large, ETFs follow indexes and are inexpensive choices.

ETFs also trade differently than mutual funds. Mutual funds generally trade only once per day and may be exclusive to one brokerage company or another. ETFs are generally available anywhere and can trade at any time of the day. For most people doing long-term investing, however, this distinction isn't important.

Options

Options fall into two basic categories: puts and calls. Puts give you the right to sell a stock at a given price, and calls give you the right to buy a stock at a given price.

You can buy or sell puts and calls on most stocks. Some people sell options as a way to make extra income, while other people buy puts and calls as a way to hedge existing investment positions or make bets on future price movements in stocks.

Option prices generally move much faster than underlying stock prices, and options can serve as a form of leverage that magnifies the movement of the underlying product.

I almost never recommend options. For one thing, they're much harder to understand than stocks. If you think a stock is going to go down, does it make more sense to sell the right for someone else to buy the stock from you in exchange for cash now, or does it make more sense to pay cash now in exchange for the right to sell the stock to someone else at a later date? Depending on whether or not you own shares of the stock involved, potential gains, losses, and risk really need to be thought through carefully.

For another thing, options are more dangerous.

If you buy a stock, it could go up or down in the short run, but if it's a good business, in the long run it'll go up in value. However, if you buy an option betting on the price of the same stock to go up, not only do you have to be right on your premise that the stock will increase in value, but you also have to be right about when it will go up in value.

That's because options expire at a certain time. Some options expire after a day, while other options expire after three years or any time in between. But even within a three-year timeframe, an excellent stock in an excellent company could go up or down in price for reasons that are varied and unpredictable, and even if your investment premise is correct in the long run, you can still lose on the option investment when it expires.

The danger is magnified by leverage. Since you're betting on the movement of a stock above or below a certain price, those differences can either make you a lot of money very fast or wipe you out very fast.

Selling options has a similar risk that might cause you to lose a large amount of money even if your underlying predictions turn out to be correct in the long run, and depending on what you do, you can even lose more money than you initially invested.

In general, most people should avoid options.

Residential real estate

Residential real estate is quite popular because it's easy for everyone to understand. Unless you're homeless, you live somewhere. Even if you are homeless, you understand that most people live somewhere. And of the people who live somewhere, many pay rent.

The idea of buying a house or condo or apartment complex and renting it to other people is really simple. As long as the rent is higher than your expenses, you make a profit, and if the property goes up in value, you can make an additional profit. Some of your profits can also be tax deferred (meaning that you don't have to pay taxes on them until later in the future) as you recognize depreciation on the property.

Residential real estate is popular for another reason: It's really easy to borrow money cheaply.

Banks love lending money for real estate purchases. The real estate secures the loan, loans generally can be resold to other banks or investors, and government regulations look favorably on real-estate loans held by banks. For banks, lending money for real estate is thought of as a low-risk option.

Although most people buy stocks with cash (you can borrow to invest in stocks with a margin loan, but the interest rates are typically higher than on real estate loans), real estate is generally purchased with debt. If everything works out and someone else puts up the capital for the property you buy, your net income is almost like money from the sky. It's great! Until it's not.

Residential real estate is not guaranteed any more than any other investment. Sometimes the properties go down in value. Sometimes the roof leaks and the air conditioning fails and you need to come up with a large amount of money for repairs. Or you might have trouble find a tenant. Or you might find a tenant who's trouble. Or Congress might pass a Coronavirus relief bill that prevents you from evicting the tenant who won't pay his rent while you're stuck paying for a mortgage and property taxes and repairs.

Borrowing money to buy residential real estate is very easy to do, but it's not a magic formula for instant wealth. It's a tool that potentially increases your payout while also increasing your risk of failure.

Real estate also has another major drawback: It requires labor. You can buy a stock or put money in the bank and never think about it again. But if you buy residential real estate, you have to start by understanding the locations and neighborhoods where you're buying. Then you need to think about the renting process, the repair and maintenance required (including the dreaded 3 a.m. phone call about the leaking toilet), and how to interact with your tenant.

Much of that can be mitigated by hiring a property manager, but a property manager isn't free, and anything that reduces the amount of labor and attention required of you is going to reduce your return on investment.

Finally, residential real estate has a liquidity challenge. While it's easy to sell a stock and get your money right away if you need it, it's not so easy to get your money out of a property. Selling the property can take a lot of time. If you didn't borrow too much when you bought the property, you could set up a line of credit with the property as collateral, but then you'd be taking on debt rather than liquidating your investment, which means increasing your risk profile.

That said, there's nothing wrong with investing in residential real estate as long as you have the time to put into it, you can make your initial purchase without having to borrow excessively, and you have other sources of cash that are easily accessible should you need them. Reasonable investments in residential real estate are much better than no investments at all. But considering the challenges as compared to stocks, I wouldn't recommend investing in residential real estate unless it's all you understand.

Commercial real estate

Commercial real estate functions much the same way as residential real estate. The only difference is that instead of renting a property to a person for a home, instead you're renting to a business or a group of businesses.

This is much more complex, and generally you need far more capital, lawyers and CPAs who can help you with leasing and tax issues, and a greater understanding of a more complex market.

If you're able to figure out capitalization rates, likely occupancy rates, and how the business climate in the area looks, as well as what a desirable business location would be, commercial real estate has the potential for generating very high rates of return.

On the other hand, if you don't understand what you're getting yourself into or if you have to borrow excessively in order to make the investment, you take on significant risks that have the potential to cause harm to your financial future.

This is an area where I would tread cautiously until you have more capital and more experience.

Annuities

Annuities are a very old investment product. They've been around since at least the time of the Roman Empire, and involve trading a lump sum of cash for a series of periodic payments.

Most common are immediate annuities issued by insurance companies, in which you give your money to the insurance company, and they make monthly or annual payments to you, usually for the rest of your life. There are many other variations that involve fixed payment periods, deferral periods, basis adjustments depending on stock market or other indexes, and so forth.

Although annuities are state-regulated insurance products and are very safe (annuity loses are extremely rare), annuities have two major drawbacks: The first is that your initial capital is either permanently lost or severely compromised, and the second is that the rate of return is very poor.

On the first point, annuities generally require that you hand over your capital to the insurance company because that's how the insurance company makes money to cover the payments they make to you. Some annuities may allow you to surrender your contract (give up your right to future payments) in exchange for a lump sum of cash to be returned to you, but you'll almost always have major surrender charges if you choose that. And, of course, when you pass away, your estate and your family receive nothing since the capital went to the issuer. This is particularly bad if you end up having a short life and receive payments for only a short time.

On the second point, the complexity of annuities as insurance products serves mostly to generate fees for the insurance company and the agent selling the product. The more complex the annuity product, the greater the fees involved. Combined with the ultra-conservative investment requirements that most insurance companies are required to hold and the very low level of interest rates those carry, and annuity almost always makes a poor investment choice.

Compounding this poor rate of return is that most annuities are not indexed for inflation. Whatever fixed payment you get will lose purchasing power over time as prices rise. Annuities that include inflation protection have lower payout rates or higher fees, so you end up losing either way.

Considering the drawbacks, would anyone ever want an annuity? Yes, but it's rare.

Only once did I ever recommend that someone purchase an annuity. It was an older person with no children who had a decades-long track record of handling money poorly, who had no investment plan for his future, and who had recently inherited a modest amount of money.

A low-return stream of income that lasts for the rest of your life is better than having a pot of money that you spend down right away and that leaves you elderly and broke. An annuity is a wonderful safety tool for a person who can't be trusted to handle his money wisely.

This person declined my advice on the annuity and decided to buy a new car instead. It was a nice car, but not a good financial decision. Unfortunately, people who aren't good with money and who would benefit from the security of owning an annuity generally aren't the sort of people who run out and buy annuities.

Besides the irresponsible, annuities can also be useful for people who want to hide assets from creditors or shield estate from taxation, but those are very complex topics that go beyond the scope of this book.

As long as you are confident in your ability to look at the money you have and save it for your future, you should walk away from annuities. But if you don't think you can trust yourself with your own money, an annuity would be something to consider by contacting your favorite insurance company for more information.

Bitcoin and commodities

Do you know what "blockchain" means? Do you understand the mechanics of cryptocurrencies? Do you understand the risks involved in holding digital assets? If so, Bitcoin and other cryptocurrencies may be for you.

If you don't know what this is about, then stay away from Bitcoin. Investing in something you don't understand is a mistake.

Even if you do understand Bitcoin, you would want to make only very small investments, if any.

Bitcoin generates no income. There is no underlying business. It is a digital asset that sits there and does nothing. There is no interest; there are no dividends. The only way you make money in Bitcoin is if someone else buys it from you for more than you paid.

That is the definition of speculation.

People make money speculating all the time. Sometimes you buy something, it goes up in value, and you sell it at a profit. It's a lot of fun when that happens. But people also lose money from speculating.

Instead, you should look for opportunities that actually generate cash flow. You want income and a real, underlying business, something producing economic value.

Commodity investing works the same way as bitcoin. If you buy wheat futures, oil futures, pork bellies, or any other standard commodity, you're not purchasing a generator of economic value; you're speculating that someone else will buy the commodity from you at a higher price.

Commodities are generally easier to understand than cryptocurrencies, but they still suffer from the same speculative drawbacks.

The only exception for commodity purchases is if it's something you actually use (e.g., an airline buying oil futures to hedge price changes on its future oil consumption), but this is almost never applicable to an individual investor.

As a rule, avoid any invest that's a speculation.

Gold

Gold functions as a commodity just like any other. It carries the same risks, and you make money on it in the same way.

Unlike other commodities, however, gold, has a special place in history. It has served as a form of money everywhere on the planet for thousands of years. Gold coins are still minted to this day (mostly for collectors), and most people would happily accept payment in gold if it's offered. And it comes in really handy if you need to make calf-shaped idol to worship.

But despite this history, there's nothing magical about gold as an investment. Sometimes it goes up. Sometimes it goes down. It doesn't generate any cash flow or economic activity. It just sits there until you sell it, hopefully for more than you paid for it.

Owning gold still can have a purpose, though. In periods of inflation, it usually increases in value and offsets some of the loss of purchasing power of the dollar. In periods of geopolitical turmoil, people go to gold as a safe haven. In the event of a total economic collapse, gold would continue to work as a form of money, useful for bribing border guards, for example.

Considering that stocks also largely go up in value during periods of inflation and that gold doesn't generate any income to help improve your financial future, the real value of gold comes as an insurance policy against total economic collapse. There's a use in that, but you don't want to go overboard.

If you were to purchase insurance against every conceivable catastrophe, you wouldn't have to fear any economic injuries, but you also wouldn't have any money left.

Buy gold only to the extent you want to diversify the money you plan to keep permanently in cash in case of a catastrophe. But for the long run, the bulk of your money should be invested in income-generating areas that do more to help you build your wealth.

Don't be afraid!

Regardless of which investment types or styles you prefer, it's important that you not be afraid to invest beyond a bank account. Saving money and building capital is a crucial part of managing your finances, but so too is getting that capital to work for you and to grow on its own.

If your capital is a good-for-nothing deadbeat who just lounges around in a checking account playing video games all day, you'll have to work twice as hard to achieve your financial goals. You want your capital to be your partner, helping you to grow and prosper so that eventually you don't have to work unless you want to.

Investing can be a bit scary, though. You work hard to earn money and pay taxes, and you sacrifice consumption now in order to save. Taking that hard-won savings and watching it evaporate in a bad investment is no fun at all. But that is precisely the reason why investments are able to generate returns beyond what a bank account can provide.

Not everybody is willing to take risk, but someone has to take the risk of losing money in order for businesses to exist. Thus, people who take that risk are compensated by receiving the reward of success when their investments thrive.

Risk-taking is a critical part of the economy, an extremely valuable one, and a misunderstood one. Dividends and interest and rent and capital gains aren't "unearned" income as they're referred to in the tax code. They are earned because you're placing your capital at risk of disappearing in a cloud of failure. Without a chance to make a profit, nobody would invest in anything. Without risk taking and investment, it would be impossible to launch businesses, create jobs, and provide goods and services people need and want. Without risk, there would be no economy.

Generally speaking, the more risk you take, the greater your potential profit. Stocks have more risk than bonds which have more risk than cash, and historically stocks returned more than bonds which returned more than cash. But risk taking should be a calm and calculated process, one in which you understand the risks you're taking and why, rather than a whirlwind of random decisions.

Take the time to understand what you're doing, how it will pay off, and how it might fail.

If you decide to buy real estate, understand that it pays off from rental cash flow, and you run risks from bad tenants, repairs, and vacancies. If you decide to buy stocks, understand that they pay off from dividends and capital gains, and you run the risk of capital losses and dividend cuts.

Once you feel comfortable that you understand how an investment or company works, and if it looks like a good idea that will persist and succeed over many years, take a chance. If you fail, that's okay.

Failure is an inevitable part of investing. You have to embrace the fact that there's no way to avoid it, and that the occasional failure won't hurt you in the long run.

While you're working to understand investments, it's important to remember that you'll never know everything. Some people won't take action until they think they know enough; they'll read a little bit and get general ideas for what they might like to do, but they never actually take any action. In the process of missing opportunities, you squander one of your biggest assets: time. You can invest later, but investing later is usually worse for your financial future than investing sooner.

Investing is all about predicting the future, which nobody knows and which nobody can ever know. If you don't understand the basics about an investment, it's okay to learn more, but once your knowledge about an investment opportunity is "good enough," you're ready to take a risk. If you still don't feel confident, then make some small investments to get a feel for how things work. If you do something out of ignorance and lose the small investment, you've purchased an education that will make you a better investor for the future. You have to start somewhere.

If someone claims to know what investments to make because

he knows what'll happen in the future, that person is lying. Someone who actually knew the future would be sitting at home investing his own portfolio and making tons of money rather than selling advice to other people.

Don't paralyze yourself with indecision. Take a risk and take action. You are your own best investment advisor.

CHAPTER 8:
HOW TO CHOOSE INVESTMENTS

The investment world is vast. Not just vast like a Cheesecake Factory menu, but absolutely, mind-bogglingly gigantic. It's an unlimited world buffet with every conceivable food on the menu. You can choose among hundreds of thousands of stocks, bonds, mutual funds, options, derivatives, real estate, and securities so obscure that only a handful of people understand them. If only dating options were so vast.

Fortunately with investing, unlike with dating, you don't have to worry about your investment opportunity suddenly remembering that it has to wash its hair and cancelling on you. Nor do you have to worry about the investment opportunity not calling you back when promised and later revealing that it has a litany of psychological problems that will plague you for the rest of your life. You especially don't have to worry about getting stuck with the wrong investment for years and listening to the investment complain every day that you're doing something wrong. The decision-making process in investing is, thankfully, unilateral. You can change your mind about which investments you like at any time without making your old investments cry.

Although investment options are numerous, you don't have to pick everything. It's like the mother who gave her son a red necktie and a blue necktie for his birthday. When the son wore the red necktie the next day, the mother said, "so you didn't like the blue one?" Except that with investing, you don't have the guilt when you pick favorites.

Just focus on the handful of choices that are appealing to you and ignore everything else. Which is also like dating, where selecting everything at once usually doesn't work out well. The favored characteristics you look for in a date will vary dramatically from person to person, but there are a few commonalities that apply to almost everyone, such as looking for someone who's a human being, alive, and not a murderous tyrant (yes, there are exceptions for everything, and, no, I won't list them all). With investments too, there are common principles that apply to almost everyone.

Avoid fixed income

Remember Billy McWasteful? Besides spending all his money and going into debt, he's also scared to take risk with his cash. He wants something safe. When he goes to a car dealer, he asks the dealer for the safest car possible.

The dealer picks out an ultra-safe model, a really grand car that never has accidents and which comes with free government insurance. It also has a top speed of 0 mph. After you buy it, it remains motionless for ten years. At the end of ten years, you can sell it and get back some of your money.

Billy is really excited to get the car because it's safe and he's an idiot.

That sounds like a joke, but in real life it's the way the bond market works. For example, you pay $10,000 for a ten-year US Treasury note with a 0.90% interest rate, you receive $90 per year on which you have to pay income taxes, and at the end of ten years, you get back your $10,000. If inflation averages even a modest 2% per year, prices rise 22% in ten years, and your safe $10,000 bond now has only $8,200 in purchasing power.

That's an awful deal, but it's not the worst bond deal out there. Some countries have government bonds with a negative interest rate, and not only do you lose purchasing power from inflation, but you also lose absolute dollars every year. Yet people still make investments like this in the name of safety.

Other bonds pay higher interest rates, sometimes even in excess of likely inflation, but generally speaking, the higher the interest rate on a bond, the greater the chances the borrower won't pay you back.

Some ten-year bonds might pay 12% interest, and getting $1,200 per year in interest on your $10,000 investment sounds great. But if the company that sold the bond goes bankrupt after two years, you've gotten only $2,400 in total interest and you lost your $10,000 in principal. That's not such a great deal.

Other variations of fixed income, like bank CDs or municipal bonds, offer the same problems of low interest in exchange for low risk, and while municipal bonds have the advantage of being tax-free in many cases, losing your money tax-free doesn't make any sense. Even Billy McWasteful knows that.

Other than cash in a checking account for short-term cash flow, or cash in a savings account for an emergency fund or near-term spending plans, anything you can leave invested for 5-10 years should be in something other than fixed income. You wouldn't buy a motionless car in the name of safety, and you shouldn't buy a motionless investment either.

Understand your investments

Everyone's talking about it. Your friends and coworkers are all investing in it. Everyone's making money and becoming rich overnight.

Whatever "it" is, if you don't know how it works or why it makes money, you should avoid it.

Buying a condo to rent out is fairly straightforward. You pay for the condo and make money from rent. Buying a commercial office building isn't so straightforward. You need to understand the commercial office space market, capitalization rates, vacancy estimates, management costs, and so forth. Buying a gold coin is easy to understand. You buy the coin, hold it, and hope it goes up in value. Buying a bitcoin is more complicated; you know it needs to go up in value, but how do you hold it and what makes the value rise?

Sometimes the complicated thing is a better investment opportunity, but if you don't know how it works or why it's better, you're better off sticking with the thing you do understand.

The same principle applies to stocks. Coca Cola sells sugar water. McDonalds sells hamburgers and McNuggets. Proctor & Gamble sells diapers and toilet paper. These companies are all very easy to understand, and there should be no question in your mind how they make money and whether or not they'll still make money in the future.

Gilead Sciences makes biopharmaceuticals. Annaly Capital makes leveraged investments in residential mortgage-backed bonds. Qualcom leverages a telecommunications patent portfolio. These business models are more difficult to understand, and it might not be immediately clear to you how they make money or if they'll still make money in the future.

Even if the hard-to-understand companies might turn out to be better investments, you should avoid them if you don't understand them. People get hurt when they buy stuff they don't understand.

In 2001, Enron was making lots of money trading energy. Nobody really understood what that meant, but they kept reporting growing profits until one day the whole company collapsed in a cloud of accounting fraud.

Pets.com had a simple business model of shipping pet food to people, but they also reported that they lost money on every sale. Nobody understood how they intended to make a profit, but people still bought their stock since it was an internet stock during the Dot-Com bubble, and everything related to the internet was making money. Pets.com went bankrupt less than a year after going public.

Twitter and Groupon are great examples of companies with easy-to-understand products, but murky business models and no clear path toward making money. Neither of those is bankrupt yet, but you'd be well advised to avoid them like Confederate cotton bonds.

As a general rule, if you don't know what a company does or how an investment works or where the profit comes from, you should move on to something else.

Stocks are usually the best choice

For most people, stocks are an ideal investment choice. That's not to say stocks are the only choice. Lots of other investment opportunities can be quite fruitful. Some financial advisors will suggest that only real estate or only stocks or only gold is the way to invest, but if it were the case that one asset class was always, and in every way, superior to all others, everyone would have figured that out long ago.

Although many types of investments can provide good returns and there is no one answer that applies universally, I will now contradict myself by saying that stocks are almost universally the ideal mix of return and risk.

Historically, stocks are the best-performing asset class over long periods of time, and that's the place you want to be. "Best-performing" means that, if you make good investments just two or three times out of five, over long periods of time you can expect to double your money every ten years or so (which is a roughly 7% rate of return), and that's better than other asset classes have done.

That's not enough to make you rich overnight, but it is enough to make you comfortable over the course of a normal career with a normal savings rate.

Stocks also have the advantage of being a passive investment. That means you make your investment, and you don't have to do anything else. This compares favorably to active investments, such as real estate, where you make your investment, and then you have to deal with the tenant who'd rather sit around using drugs than working and paying his rent, while you discover both that the eviction process in your town takes ten months and the roof on the house is leaking and causing mold problems.

Maybe you'll get lucky and the leaky roof will turn out to be a cheap fix, or the drug-using tenant will leave and be replaced by his drug dealer, who, while perhaps not as ideal a tenant as a neurologist, at least is an entrepreneur who makes enough money to pay the rent. In either case, you've got a lot of stress ahead of you.

Active investments aren't automatically bad, but they do take up a lot of time, and time is a precious commodity while you're working and accumulating capital.

So why hasn't everyone realized that stocks are an ideal asset class for long term investments and rushed into the market? Because people fear losing money. Because they get trapped in uncertainty about whether or not they're making the right decision or if they know enough. Because they spend all their time waiting for the right stock or mutual fund or for the right opportunity to buy or sell. Because people rarely see beyond tomorrow, let alone decades into the future.

Uncertainty and fear keep people out of the stock market, and because they're out of the stock market, better returns are available for you.

Uncertainty and fear are very real features of stock investments, and there's no way to get around that. The idea of losing money in stocks is scary, especially when you're starting out and you don't have the personal experience to see that stocks rise more often than they fall over long periods of time. The great thing about losses when you're starting out is that you generally have the least capital to invest, and those losses aren't going to have a big impact on your future.

For example, if you have $1,000 to invest when you're 23 and you make a foolish choice, all you lose is the $1,000. If you're 65 and you have $1 million in investments, the stakes are much higher, but at that point you should have decades of experience behind you, and the odds of making a foolish mistake are much less.

A lot of people also confuse the idea of losing money with volatility. Stocks go up and down in the short run, seemingly at random, and you can watch the value of your portfolio bounce around in real time. It's exciting when it goes up, scary when it goes down, and the short-term movements are always accompanied by histrionic headlines in the press promising that we've entered a period of perpetual prosperity or a permanent economic depression.

Volatility isn't something to be scared of. Over long periods of time, stocks almost uniformly go up, and the fear of that short-term volatility is the very reason why stocks provide an excellent long-term return: the price of an investment is cheaper when people are scared of it. Further, short-term price fluctuations have no impact on you while you're in your asset accumulation phase of life, and when you're in retirement, volatility doesn't make a difference as long as you're not overly aggressive in consuming your retirement assets.

You can wash away much of the investment fear once you realize that finding a perfect investment or a perfect time to buy or sell is nearly impossible, and that no amount of research or planning will enable you to tell the future. Similarly, no investment professional knows the future any better than you do. Some of your investments are going to fail no matter how hard you try, and if none of your investments fail, it means you're not investing aggressively enough.

To some extent, you can mitigate this uncertainty in three ways: diversification, dollar cost averaging, and time.

You might see that Amazon.com stock keeps going higher every day. It seems like it'll go up forever, so you buy only Amazon stock. If it keeps going up forever, you're a big winner! If it stops going up, or goes down, not so much. You're entire financial fate rests on Amazon.

Diversification means simply not putting all your money in a single investment, and not relying on all your investment income coming from one place. This isn't as much fun or as exciting as making only one or two bets, but while risk is the source of long-term investment gains, the risks you take have to be calculated and reasonable.

Betting your entire net worth on the pass line of the craps table is a high-risk move with a potentially-high payoff, but you'd be a fool to place that bet. Risk should be measured and controlled, with smaller bets in many different places (and preferably not at a casino, unless it's either for fun or if you're James Bond and you have to beat the bad guy at cards in order to stop him from destroying the world).

This applies to any set of investments, not just stocks. If you want to invest in real estate, you should buy several units to spread the risk of vacancies and defaults. If you want to buy stocks, buy at least 20 different companies in different industries to reduce your risk when a company performs poorly. You don't have to get everything right. A few failures won't derail your plans if you diversify since you'll likely have a few successes to offset them.

Unfortunately, I can't tell you exactly what to buy. I don't know what sorts of things you understand or like best, and I don't know what's going to happen in the future. But I can tell you that the odds are in your favor with stocks over long periods of time, and if you make broad investments, the exact details aren't as important as simply being invested.

People have conducted studies of professional stock pickers vs. monkeys throwing darts at lists of stocks, and the results are that the monkeys typically do as well as the experts.

If you have the confidence in yourself to take a chance on managing your own investments, you can avoid the massive fees investment managers charge, which is likely to improve your long-run returns even further.

There are a couple other things you can do to improve your returns.

The first is to avoid trying too hard. While it's good to be interested in your investments, hyperactivity can be harmful in the long run. That is to say, once you've made your investment decisions, it's generally best to sit back and do nothing with them unless something significant changes with the companies in which you've invested.

Very often people will see prices falling, and they sell in a panic because they fear the prices will fall forever. Or they see prices rising, and they buy at excessively-high prices expecting prices to rise forever. In reality, prices neither rise nor fall forever, and trading as if they do is a mistake. Other times people buy and sell the same things over and over, trying to get their investment timing perfect or to make their investments "better," but nobody can know what the perfect timing is for an investment any more than anyone can know what a perfect investment is.

Studies have shown that people who trade aggressively typically do worse than people who buy and then do nothing.

The other thing you can do to improve returns is to be mindful of your purchase price. The purchase price determines whether or not you're making a good investment.

For example, you see a house for sale, and you calculate you could rent it out for $20,000 per year. Is that a good investment? It depends on the price.

If you could buy the house for $100,000, it'd be a fantastic investment generating a return of 20% per year. If the house cost $2 million, on the other hand, it would be a terrible investment yielding only 1% per year.

In both cases, it's the same house with the same cash flow. The only difference is the purchase price.

In another example, you might have a really great company like Amazon.com. Is it a good investment? If you buy it for $1,000 per share, it might be a great investment that doubles or triples in ten years. If you buy it for $5,000 per share, it might be a horrible investment that loses value in ten years.

It's the same, great company in both cases, but your investment is either wonderful or horrible depending on your purchase price.

There's no absolute rule about where to draw the line between a good price and a bad price, but as a starting point, you want to think about the dividends or cash flow you might receive, as well as the earnings of the company or business. If you're satisfied with the price you're paying for those, you'll probably be satisfied with your investment returns. For example, if a stock pays a safe 5% dividend and you're happy with that, you'll probably do okay.

If you're unsatisfied with cash flow of the investment, such as the $2 million house that generates only $20,000 per year in net income, but you're hoping it'll go up to $3 million so you can sell it to someone else and make a profit, then you're speculating, not investing. You might be able to sell at a profit to someone who also doesn't care about the poor investment cash flow, and your buyer might be able to turn around and sell at an even higher price to someone else.

Everyone involved knows the underlying investment has bad cash flow and that it's foolish to buy, but you're confident that there's a greater fool out there who will pay even more in the future. Sometimes it works out, but sometimes you're the greater fool. In speculation, you'll probably be disappointed with how things turn out.

Sometimes you're not sure what price you want to pay for something. Maybe a stock is very volatile, bouncing up and down like crazy, maybe you're just not good at calculating discounted projected cash flows in your head, or maybe you're trying to hedge your risk since markets can jump from overvalued to undervalued on a whim.

This leads to the second way to minimize investment uncertainty: dollar cost averaging. "Dollar cost averaging" means making periodic investments instead of a lump-sum investment. For example, if you want to invest $10,000, rather than investing everything in one go and hoping to get a good price, you might instead invest $1,000 per month for ten months. You'll pay more for some of the shares you buy, but other shares will be cheaper. By spreading your purchases over time, you don't have to worry as much about missing a boom or getting caught in a crash.

Without realizing it, many people use dollar cost averaging by default. When you make monthly 401(k) contributions, every month, year after year, or annual IRA contributions, you're spreading out your stock purchases over months and years, reducing your risk on the initial purchase timing.

In many ways, dollar cost averaging is like dating: They both start with "d" and end with "ing," so that's something. But other than that, dating and dollar-cost-averaging are nothing alike.

Finally, you can mitigate investment risk through the application of time.

In the short run, stocks can bounce up and down seemingly at random. Short-term trading can result in quick profits and quick losses in a highly-competitive environment that's 90% dominated by automated trading systems and sophisticated investment companies. In the short run, you don't have any advantage at all as an investor. Anything could happen.

The long run, by which I mean 5-10 years or more, is a different story. In the long run, stocks generally rise. You might have a bad year every now and then as you invest, but if you can extend your investment horizon to include more years, the odds move more and more in your favor as the timeline grows. The long run is where you, the individual investor, have the biggest advantages: 1) long-term investments historically produce the most consistent, positive returns, and 2) there is no automated trading program anywhere that would buy an investment and hold it for ten or twenty years. You have the power to do something that a computer can't do, and you can profit from that.

Mutual funds as an alternate choice

Maybe number crunching isn't your thing. Many things aren't my "thing" either, including sports, broccoli, and My Little Pony episodes, which, as the father of two girls, I had to endure in quantities far beyond those allowed under the Geneva Convention.

If that's the case, there's nothing wrong with making your stock investments in broad-based index funds that give you exposure to the whole stock market, such as S&P 500 index funds from companies like Vanguard which gives you instant exposure to the 500 largest companies in the S&P 500 index. You could also pick out mutual funds or other managed investments where someone else selects baskets of investments on your behalf.

If you want to go the route of paying to have your investments managed or selected for you, there's a very simple metric that lets you know whether the fund will likely perform well or perform poorly. That's the expense ratio.

Funds that charge very high annual management fees almost always do worse than funds that charge very low management fees, at least when both funds have similar sorts of investments. It's not hard to understand why.

The stock market overall is made up of everyone. That's what determines the average return; you just add everyone together. If you divide up all the stocks in the market into different mutual fund pools, you'll still have the same average return because you haven't actually changed anything. All the mutual funds are, on average, going to have average returns, because when you add them all together, you get everyone.

However, every mutual fund charges a management fee. They need to pay for administration, regulatory compliance, customer service, marketing, and offices. An average fund with a high management fee is going to leave you with less money than an average fund with a low management fee. It's impossible to pay management fees and to have everyone be above average.

There are certainly exceptions. Some funds are going to be above average for long periods of time, even with their fees. But I guarantee you won't be able to identify them in advance, because neither you nor anyone else knows the future. You can guess that because a fund did well in the past, it might do well in the future. And it might do well, but there's no guarantee.

If you take a group of 100,000 mutual funds, 50,000 of them will be in the top 50% in any given year, by definition. Out of those 50,000 funds, 25,000 funds will be in the top 50% the following year. And 12,500 will be in the top the year after that. After 15 years, you'll have three mutual funds that were in the top 50% every single year over that period.

Maybe it'll be because they know something, but more likely it's just random chance. Are those three funds going to be in the top 50% for the 16th year? Maybe, but they could just as easily end up in the bottom 50%.

But let's say, hypothetically, that there's one magical fund manager in existence. One person who really gets it. One person who predicts with 100% accuracy what's going to happen next. And let's say that this person likes managing money for people and isn't just retired on an island somewhere.

Once people realize that this one person is always right, money will start pouring into his mutual fund. The fund will grow larger and larger to the point that, whenever he's ready to make an investment, the very act of his investing will cause the price of that investment to rise.

Since the return from an investment decreases as the purchase price rises, every time this magical manager makes an investment, the return from his investment will collapse from the rising price, and he'll no longer be able to outperform the market.

Magical money management based on knowing the future can work only if nobody knows that you know the future and you operate on a small enough scale not to affect the market. Therefore, if such a person were to exist, either you would never find him, or, if you found him, his returns would crash as a result of having been found.

The point of all this is that you should go into mutual-fund purchases expecting average performance, and you should focus primarily on getting the lowest fee possible in order to maximize the amount of the return you get to keep.

Leverage

One of the most powerful tools in successful investing is the application of time. The more time you put in, the greater your gain is likely to be. But there's a problem: Waiting is really, really boring.

Some people try to get around that by leveraging their investments with debt. You could borrow money against your house or on a credit card, or, more commonly, you could borrow money on margin with your stocks as the collateral. With the extra cash on hand, you can buy more stocks and make things move faster.

For example, if you buy 10 shares of Amazon at $3,000 per share, you invest $30,000. If it later goes up to $4,000 per share, your investment is worth $40,000, a profit of $10,000.

However, if you borrow against your initial Amazon shares, you could take your initial $30,000 in cash, borrow $30,000 more, and buy

20 shares of Amazon worth $60,000. If the price goes up to $4,000, you'll have $80,000 worth of shares. Once you sell and pay back the $30,000 you borrowed, you'll have turned your $30,000 into $50,000, a $20,000 profit.

Borrowing to invest is called "leverage." Leverage is a very powerful tool that can magnify your gains and grow your money faster. But there's also an added risk involved.

In the Amazon example, once you borrow $30,000 to get your 20 shares, what happens if the price goes down to $2,000 instead of going up? Now, your 20 shares are worth $40,000, and after you sell and pay back your $30,000 loan, you have only $10,000 left out of your original $30,000 in cash. You've lost $20,000.

Imagine instead the price went to $1,000 per share. Now you'd have $20,000 worth of shares and $30,000 worth of debt. You'd have lost everything, and you'd still owe $10,000 to your broker for the stock you no longer own.

Borrowing money to invest helps you to gain money faster, and it also helps you to lose money faster. It definitely makes things more exciting.

More often than not, stocks will go up rather than down, so more often than not, leveraging your investments will help you to make money faster rather than losing money faster. But leverage can go very quickly from a blessing to a curse and it can very quickly cause enormous amounts of stress. That stress can then lead to decision making based on short-term price fluctuations which is contrary to all the investing advantages you have over the long term. I highly recommend avoiding borrowed money for investments.

CHAPTER 9:
MINIMIZING TAXES

Once upon a time, there was a magical fairy who enjoyed paying taxes. She flew around a magical forest visiting her magical friends, and every 15 minutes she gave magical fairy dust to the insatiable magical government. Nothing made her happier than demands for fairy dust, and the more fairy dust the magical government demanded, the happier the magical fairy became.

She didn't care that the magical government wasted the magical fairy dust on one program for growing a magical forest and another program for burning down the forest. As long as she paid her taxes, she was happy.

Does the magical fairy sound like you? I didn't think so.

Unless you have self-destructive tendencies, paying taxes does nothing but act as a deadweight loss on your path to financial progress, and you want to do everything you can to get that massive expense to be more manageable. Unfortunately, after several decades of tax-code changes, there aren't many legal tax shelters remaining for people who have regular jobs, with the notable exception of retirement savings.

The various types of retirement plans give you ways to defer taxes or avoid them completely, and if you make optimal contributions to these accounts, you'll be able to lower your long-term tax bill significantly.

If you haven't yet built an emergency fund or gotten your debts under control, you'll want to tackle those tasks first. Tax efficiency is great, but not if you're unable to pay for a surprise car repair or if you're paying 29% interest on a credit card. But assuming that's not an issue for you, here's the order in which your accounts should be funded to minimize long-term taxes. If you're not eligible for one of these accounts, just skip to the next one:

1. 401(k) or 403(b) plan up to the maximum company match
2. Health savings account
3. Roth IRA
4. 401(k) or 403(b) up to the annual limit
5. Taxable investments.

If you have a company match available to you, that's one of the biggest financial gifts you can receive. Your employer is basically handing you free money in exchange for you saving for your future, which you should be doing anyway. If the match is 100%, every dollar you contribute to your 401(k) gets an effective 100% instant return, which you'll never find anywhere else. Even if the company offers a 50% match or a 30% match, you'll never beat that.

Even better, money contributed by an employer directly to your 401(k) is not subject to income taxes until you withdraw it in retirement, and it's never subject to Social Security and Medicare taxes, which is another 7.65% instant return.

Next, you should fully fund your health savings account (HSA) if you have one. The HSA is quadruple tax advantaged: 1) Contributions to the HSA are not subject to federal or state income taxes; 2) contributions are not subject to Social Security and Medicare taxes (oddly, this benefit applies only to employees who contribute through payroll withholding, not to people who contribute independently); 3) investment earnings are not subject to income taxes; and 4) withdrawals for medical expenses are not subject to income taxes.

You'll never find an account anywhere with better tax treatment, and you should fund this account to the maximum each year. If you are fortunate enough not to need the money, there's no downside to overfunding your HSA. Unused balances belong to you and roll over from year to year. Withdrawals after age 65 for non-medical purposes are subject to ordinary income taxes, but there are no penalty taxes at that age. In effect, an overfunded HSA works just like a traditional IRA or 401(k), but with the added bonus of tax-free withdrawals for medical expenses.

Once your HSA is fully funded, you'll want to contribute to your Roth IRA and your spouse's Roth IRA. There's always the debate about whether it's better to pay taxes now or pay taxes later, but I firmly believe that it's almost always better to pay the taxes now and fund the Roth. There are three reasons for this.

First, most people have larger 401(k) balances than Roth IRA balances. That's simply because the 401(k) has a much higher contribution limit and it often receives employer matching contributions. Much the same way that it's important to reduce your investment risk through diversification, it's also important to reduce your future tax risk through tax diversification.

If you have some money in your 401(k) plan, you know you'll have to pay taxes on withdrawals in the future. But if you also have a Roth IRA, you'll have a separate pot of money you can access tax free. Depending on your tax situation in the future, this gives you options and choices, which is exceedingly valuable.

The second reason for choosing a Roth IRA over a traditional IRA is the higher effective contribution limit. Both accounts have a $6,000 contribution limit, but $6,000 in a Roth will grow into a pot of money for retirement that won't have any deductions for retirement income taxes, whereas $6,000 in a traditional IRA or 401(k) will grow into a pot of money that generates many future tax bills.

Effectively, the immediate tax-deduction you give up by funding the Roth account becomes an additional contribution into the account, which can grow tax free over potentially many decades.

Third, the Roth account has greater flexibility for early withdrawals. Although you can make hardship withdrawals at early ages from traditional IRAs and 401(k) plans, the Roth accounts have an added feature which allows you to withdraw your after-tax contributions without any tax liability (this applies just to your contributions; there's a penalty for early withdrawal of investment earnings).

Obviously, you want to minimize early withdrawals from retirement accounts if at all possible, but it's very helpful to have that option just in case.

Next, you should fully fund your 401(k) or 403(b) plan. Although the Roth IRA is preferable to the 401(k), once you've fully funded your Roth IRA you need somewhere else to put additional tax-advantaged savings. Deferring the taxes on your contributions to the 401(k) is a great opportunity to help you grow your wealth, and while it is still subject to Medicare and Social Security taxes, the $19,500 contribution limit allows you to defer taxes on quite a lot of your money, especially if you're married and both spouses can contribute. This is particularly valuable for high-income earners who are both in high tax brackets and potentially ineligible, based on income, to contribute to a Roth IRA.

Finally, if you still have additional money to invest in your future, you should contribute to a taxable investment account. This won't provide you with any special deductions, and you'll have to pay income taxes on your dividends and capital gains. But for most people, dividends and capital gains are subject to a 15% tax rate, which is far lower than the tax rate paid on ordinary wages. Even better, there's no tax due on capital gains until you sell your investments, which gives you a great deal of control on when you pay the tax.

You'll notice that saving for your kids' college funds is not on this list, whether in a tax-advantaged 529 account or some other type. Helping your kids pay for college without having to take on debt is a wonderful goal. If you want to prioritize this at all, it should be last on your list for a the very practical reason that your kids can borrow money to go to college, but if your retirement fund is a little short, nobody is going to give you a loan to walk away from work.

While there are a few different types of accounts that have some tax benefits for kids' college savings, most of the tax benefits are minimal. College savings should be done as part of your taxable investment accounts for the reasons of simplicity and flexibility, simplicity because it's one less account to think about, and flexibility because you can use the money for yourself in case of emergency. You also have the flexibility to use it to help your kids fund a house or business if the kids are able to get college scholarships or come across other opportunities that make more sense.

Most people, of course, don't have enough money left over to fully fund every account available, and that's okay. You don't have to save $60,000 per year to provide for your future. Just do the best you can and contribute as much money as you can to each of the accounts on this list, starting from the first one, and working your way down.

For people with businesses

If you happen to have a business, you get an additional retirement option that isn't available to regular employees: the SEP-IRA. The SEP-IRA works just like a 401(k) plan, but the limits are much higher. You may contribute up to 20% of your net business income or $57,000, whichever is lower. It's an extremely high limit, and while it's not clear what the rationale is for preventing regular employees from having access to that much tax-sheltering capacity, this is just the way the tax code is written.

If your net business income is less than $285,000, you won't be able to use the full $57,000 contribution limit on the SEP-IRA, but there's a workaround if you still want to save more than 20% of your net income: a solo 401(k) plan. That works the same way as a regular 401(k) plan, except that you're the only participant. It allows you to contribute the full $19,500 "employee" contribution allowed under regular 401(k) plans, and you can also contribute up to 20% of your net business income as an "employer" contribution, up to the total aggregate limit of $57,000.

For example, if your net business income is $150,000, you can contribute $19,500 as an "employee" plus $30,000 as the "employer" for a total contribution of $49,500.

Solo 401(k) plans generally have higher fees than SEP-IRA plans, so the SEP-IRA would be the one to utilize first, but the solo 401(k) can give you much greater contribution flexibility depending on how much net income your business generates and how much you're able to save.

Really, it's pretty silly to have so many types of retirement plans available in so many different variations, and it's even more silly to have different limits based solely on whether you're self-employed or just an employee. The more sensible thing would be to have traditional and Roth IRA limits set at $57,000 for everyone and to get rid of all the other plans and limits, but such is not consistent with the wisdom of our 535 omniscient Congressional supermen.

So, as long as we live in this mishmash world of retirement-plan nonsense, at least you have options for protecting your money, even if it's not always an elegant solution.

For everyone

Adjust your withholding. Although the benefit is relatively small, you can improve your tax situation by optimizing your withholding elections out of your paycheck or your estimated tax payments if you're self-employed.

The government has a really neat income tax system set up: You have to guess what you're income is going to be in the future, and pay your taxes now. If you guess too high and overpay your taxes, you get a refund without interest, and if you guess too low and underpay your taxes, you get a tax bill and a bonus penalty. To the best of my knowledge, this is the only area in the tax code where failure to be clairvoyant is a punishable offense.

Most people simply set their tax withholding too high, don't think about it, and celebrate when they get a refund after filing their taxes. Aside from the interest that's lost on your overpaid taxes (which, admittedly, isn't that much in the current environment of 0% interest), that big refund check often feels like free money from the sky, and people have a tendency to waste money that doesn't feel directly connected to their labors, even if the money is their own.

You don't want to waste your own money. Try to estimate how much your tax bill is going to be. If your income is likely to be the same as last year, look at your prior-year tax return and check the line for your actual taxes. Then adjust your withholding to match that tax bill.

If this results in a slightly larger paycheck, you're going in the right direction. You should then take those extra dollars and apply them to debt repayment or savings or investments. The key is to avoid spending more, which is counterproductive when your goal is to build wealth, and it's often much easier to avoid spending more when you deal with small amounts of money on a frequent basis rather than a large amount of money once per year.

Plus, tax overpayments that eventually get refunded to you are your money, and there's no reason why you shouldn't have immediate access to your own money.

Workplace tax shelters. Beyond the normal 401(k) and health savings account (HSA) plans, there are some other ways to save on taxes on a regular salary. There aren't a lot of these, but for people with predictable expenses and certain workplace plans available, you can cut your tax bill with minimal downside.

If you have children and childcare expenses, you can put up to $5,000 per year into a dependent-care flexible spending account (FSA). This is a use-it-or-lose-it deal, but it's generally quite easy to spend $5,000 on daycare. The money goes into the FSA from your paycheck, and it goes out to pay your eligible expenses. If you're in the 22% Federal tax bracket, 5% for state taxes, and 7.65% for Social Security and Medicare taxes, this would save you $1,733 per year.

Similarly, if you are fairly certain you'll spend $2,750 or more on unreimbursed medical, dental, and vision expenses (or, if you have an HSA, $2,750 just on dental and vision expenses), a medical FSA (or limited-purpose medical FSA for people who already have an HSA) is another use-it-or-lose-it plan that can cut your taxes by $953. Like the childcare FSA, money goes into the account directly from your paycheck and before your taxes are calculated, and it goes out to reimburse you for eligible medical, dental, and vision costs.

Commuting expenses may not be deductible, but if you spend up to $270 per month on mass transit, or up to $270 per month on parking, you can contribute to a section 132(f) plan. Contributions to this plan come from your paycheck and get paid out to cover your mass transit or parking expenses. Like the FSA plans, this is also a use-it-or-lose-it plan, but you have the option to change your contribution each month. You also have the option to contribute $270 for mass transit and $270 for parking, and if you use the maximum amount each month, you'll save $2,245 per year in taxes.

With all of these plans, the critical consideration is that you know in advance how much you'll spend. The tax savings are wasted if you don't use the money in the account and forfeit the remainder. But if you can take advantage of the opportunity to cut your tax bill, you help yourself without giving up anything.

Generate more income. This is counterintuitive, but sometimes you can reduce your taxes by reporting *more* income and paying *more* taxes. There are two main cases where this comes into play: non-refundable tax credits and tax-bracket arbitrage.

The first is easiest to understand. Some tax credits are not refundable, or have only limited refundability. For example, the child tax credit is $2,000 per child, but if you don't owe any taxes, the child tax credit is refundable only up to $1,400. If you have three children, but limited taxable income, you'll receive only $4,200 in child tax credits instead of the full $6,000.

The simplest way to maximize your child tax credit is to have more income. That might mean trying to get a bonus or earn more money this year instead of next year. Or, if you have money in a 401(k) or traditional IRA, you could do a Roth IRA conversion to increase your taxable income.

If you're in the 12%, married tax bracket earning $64,000 per year and with three kids, you'll use $4,200 of your child tax credit with nothing left to refund to you. However, if you also do a $15,000 Roth IRA conversion, your tax bill goes up by $1,800 while your child tax credit also goes up by $1,800. Presto! You just did a tax-free Roth IRA conversion, and you'll never owe taxes on that $15,000 or its investment income for the rest of your life.

Tax bracket arbitrage, on the other hand, is a little more difficult to understand.

The general approach to traditional IRAs and 401(k) plans is to shelter as much taxable income as possible immediately, and that's a good starting point. But eventually the tax comes due when you take withdrawals in retirement. The deferral is good, but if your retirement tax bracket is the same as your working tax bracket, you haven't really accomplished anything vs. using a Roth IRA. Paying 20% of the seed is the same as paying 20% of the harvest.

The traditional IRA makes sense only if your retirement tax bracket is lower than your working tax bracket. That's often the case by default, but why settle for default when you can lock in a low tax bracket?

If you're in the 12% tax bracket during your career and you contribute to your 401(k), you save 12% in taxes. If, in retirement, your wife decides to remodel the kitchen, your daughter gets married, your car goes kaput and your roof needs replacing, and you also get divorced, which, besides being expensive, also puts you into higher, single tax brackets, the $150,000 you might have to pull out of your retirement accounts suddenly gets taxed at 32%. Even if you can afford the expense, you just lost 20% more in taxes on your withdrawal than you saved on your contributions, which is the opposite of what you want.

On the other hand, there's no reason you can't plan ahead. Particularly for retired people who have great control over their taxable income, you should Roth convert as much of your traditional IRA and 401(k) as you can to lock in the 10% and 12% tax brackets, and you should do this every year.

For example, a retired, married couple earning $60,000 per year in Social Security and pension income is in the 12% tax bracket. That bracket continues up to $105,000 per year in gross income. By doing a $45,000 Roth IRA conversion, the couple pays 12% in taxes now, and $0 in taxes in the future.

After doing that for a few years, if a time comes when the couple needs $150,000 all at once, they suddenly have no need to fear the 32%

tax bracket because the whole thing was previously taxed at 12%. They won't owe anything else.

This kind of strategy works best if your income happens to be much lower in one year than what it typically is, or if you're retired and you can control your taxable income to make it whatever you want. In some cases you might even be willing to put yourself in the 22% tax bracket, but at the very least you're probably well served taking full advantage of the 10% and 12% brackets since it's doubtful you'll pay less than that in the future.

<u>Avoid capital gains taxes</u>. If you have appreciated assets in a taxable brokerage account, selling them could trigger capital gains taxes. You don't want to pay those. Unlike most income, capital gains income is tax advantaged in two ways: the rates are lower, and you control when you realize that income.

Much like tax-bracket arbitrage, you should take advantage of the lowest capital gains brackets. Generally, this applies only to assets held for one year or longer.

For a married couple, you pay 0% tax on capital gains as long as your total income is under $105,000, and you'd be a fool not to take advantage of that every year. If you have $50,000 in other income (whether from a job, social security, dividends, etc.), you can realize up to $55,000 in long-term capital gains without paying any federal income tax. That doesn't mean you have to sell stocks you want to keep. Instead, just sell, realize the gain, and buy back 5 seconds later.

Although there are rules against deducting capital losses on assets you immediately buy back ("wash sales"), those rules don't apply to gains. Magically, your capital gain tax bill disappeared!

If you're in a higher tax bracket, capital gains taxes are 15% up to $250,000 of income, vs. 18.8% up to $500,000 and 23.8% over that. Depending on your circumstances, maybe it would make sense to realize taxes at 15% to avoid a 23.8% tax later on, but if you're on good terms with your parents or your children, you might have other options to avoid the tax altogether.

If you have a parent who's 100 years old and very ill, and if you are the only beneficiary of his estate (or if the estate documents are very well organized so you won't be fighting with other beneficiaries), you could give your highly appreciated stocks to your parent. When your parent passes away, you inherit your stocks back, but the cost basis is stepped up to that from the date of death. Tada! Capital gains are gone.

Alternatively, if you're the 100-year-old parent, the first call you make from your deathbed should be to your stockbroker with instructions to sell all of your positions showing a tax loss to the extent it offsets any realized gains you have, and to give all remaining, unrealized tax-loss positions to your children. If you pass away with unrealized capital losses, those die with you, and it's extremely helpful if you can pass along those losses to someone who can use them.

Itemize deductions. Lastly, you can tinker a bit with itemizing deductions. After the Trump tax cuts, there's really not much benefit anymore to itemizing for most people since the standard deduction is so high and the state and local tax limits are quite low. However, if you're close to the point where your itemized deductions would exceed the standard deduction, you can benefit by bunching together your deductions into the current year.

For example, if you usually give $10,000 per year to charity, you could instead donate $30,000 in the current year and $0 for the next two years. You're still giving away just as much money, but you suddenly have $20,000 in extra deductions for the current year, money which might have otherwise been non-deductible due to your total itemized deductions coming in under the standard deduction.

Similarly, if you can prepay mortgage interest this year instead of paying on schedule next year, you increase your mortgage-interest deduction this year.

Calculating your itemized deductions and paying more in advance vs. taking the standard deduction isn't always a simple process for tax planning purposes, and if you don't understand what's involved in this process, it's better not to bother, as is often the case for most things you don't understand.

While the benefit of grouping itemized deductions into the current year has the potential to be significant, often the benefit is much smaller than you might expect (or it might be no benefit at all), and if you're not sure which is the case for you, you don't have to feel bad about not maximizing your itemized deductions. You might not actually be missing out.

Tax strategies that are not helpful

People often talk about the wonderful tax benefits that come from owning a house. In 1980, when mortgage interest was 16% and the top tax rate was 70%, buying a house was a huge tax saver. The enormous interest deduction and the very high percentage you saved in tax combined in a way that was hard to beat. But now, with interest rates very low, you're not paying all that much interest in the first place, which means there isn't much to deduct, and tax rates are much lower.

Not only that, but the doubling of the standard deduction under the Trump tax cuts, combined with a $10,000 cap on deductions for state and local taxes, means that the net benefit on your taxes from buying a home is quite small.

Let's look at an example of a married couple earning $100,000 per year. Let's say they buy a house for $300,000 with a 3% mortgage and no money down. Interest on the mortgage is $9,000. Let's say they also pay $6,000 in property tax and $7,000 in state income tax.

The state and local taxes are $13,000 total, but only $10,000 is deductible. The $9,000 in mortgage interest is deductible, for a total of $19,000 in itemized deductions. Since the standard deduction is $24,800, which they get regardless of their itemized total, the net tax benefit from buying the house is $0.

Let's look at another couple that makes $300,000 per year and buys a $700,000 house with a 3% mortgage and no money down. Mortgage interest would be $21,000. Property taxes might be $20,000, and state income taxes might be $20,000.

Their $40,000 in state and local taxes is capped at $10,000 for deductibility, and combined with $21,000 in mortgage interest, they have $31,000 in itemized deductions.

Itemizing is great, but you lose the standard deduction of $24,800 when you do that, which leaves them with a net benefit of $6,200 in additional deductions. $300,000 of income puts them in the 24% tax bracket, but let's say it's 30% with state taxes.

Thus, the net tax benefit for this couple in buying a house is $1,860. That's nice, but for a couple earning $300,000 with a $700,000 house, it's not enough money to be relevant. My advice: If you buy a house, buy it because you can afford it and it works for your personal situation. Expect little to no tax benefits in the process, no matter what your realtor tells you.

Here's another tax strategy that's counterproductive: children. Children come with a $2,000 child tax credit for most people. That's a really great tax savings. But the cost of raising a child is far in excess of $2,000 per year (unless you are aiming to be a deadbeat parent or to send the kids out to work on the farm, which I don't recommend), so the child becomes a net financial loss.

That's not to say children aren't great (especially my own children, who are perfect and without flaw, unlike everyone else's kids), but if people tell you that children are good for tax purposes, while that's correct, you shouldn't have children and expect to come out ahead financially.

Charitable giving is another way to reduce taxes. But like buying a house, the tax savings are likely to be much smaller than you think. In the example of the first couple earning $100,000 per year and buying a house, if they gave away $5,000 to charity, the net tax benefit for them would still be $0. If they gave away $10,000, they would net a $4,200 tax deduction, but they'd be in the 12% federal tax bracket and would save only $500.

The bottom line in the tax code is that it's pretty straight forward, and Congress has taken away most of the options for creativity. If you hear from someone that he has a remarkable strategy for lowering your taxes (especially if it's someone like a realtor who's trying to sell you something), chances are it's not going to work. Generally, the more complicated the strategy, the less likely it is to work. So take advantage of the easy ways to save on taxes, and make life simple.

CHAPTER 10:
THE IMPORTANCE OF SAVING

I knew someone who was a successful orthodontist. He had a wonderful house, a vacation home at the beach, a new Mercedes, and a fairly expensive lifestyle. This was a person with a good life. He enjoyed his job and worked into his 80's, and after six decades of installing braces, you can imagine how much money he accumulated.

Then a funny thing happened. When he passed away, his wife, who never was involved in the finances, discovered that her husband leased the Mercedes, mortgaged his house and vacation home until there was no equity remaining, and left her not just bereft of a spouse, and not just without any money, but also with a giant pile of debt.

Some people have a strategy to spend everything by the time they die so they can enjoy every last cent, and this orthodontist took that philosophy a step further by enjoying borrowed money too. You might look upon him as an example of success, enjoying his money to the maximum before he died, especially if he didn't like his wife much and was delighted at the prospect of dumping a massive debt on her when he wasn't going to be around to listen to her complaining.

But for most people, this is not a viable strategy. For one thing, many people don't hate their wives, or they want to leave a legacy to their families. For another, not everybody can work into his 80's.

Then there's the possibility of ending up in heaven only to discover that your wife can track you down and complain for eternity about the debt you left her. Some scenarios are just too horrible to imagine; that's where savings come into the picture.

Savings are vital for many reasons, and not just for trying to avoid the risk of an eternity with an angry wife (although that is a pretty important reason for saving). Savings are the basis of building the wealth you need to get through retirement (you can't invest what you don't save), and the salve to get you through the downturns and surprise expenses in life.

You might think this is as obvious as the sky being blue or grass making a horrible Thanksgiving side dish, but people sure don't act like it's obvious. I'm not a fan of communists, but Leon Trotsky got one thing right: "Old age is the most unexpected of all things that can happen to a man." People act as if they'll never become old, as if they'll never need to be financially independent, as if there's always more time later to start planning for the future. Eventually, the future catches up with you.

Worse than that, people have a habit of assuming the car will never break down, the roof will never leak, the economy will never have a downturn, and nobody will ever lose a job. Over long periods of time, reality always gets in the way. You might find you're not able to work for 40 years like you originally planned. Maybe you're not able to save 20% of your income. Perhaps your investments will generate returns under 7%, or inflation could be higher than expected.

Perhaps there exists a person somewhere who will never experience an emergency or a time in his life that's financially difficult, but to plan your life around the hope of nothing bad ever happening would be ludicrous. And yet, despite the near 100% certainty that at some point in the future you'll have a need for additional money, people consistently fail to save.

There are many reasons for this, but the two main reasons are 1) that people assume that the way things are now is the way things are going to be forever, and 2) lack of money.

The first reason is simply a psychological flaw in the way people perceive the future. Extrapolating trends into the future has its uses, but once you acknowledge to yourself that things won't always be as they are, you open yourself up to improving your finances.

The second reason is a little more difficult to overcome, but it comes down primarily to a question of reviewing your lifestyle preferences and choosing to prioritize saving money over something you could have now. No matter how little you earn, there's always room to save. Some of those choices may be unpleasant (e.g., use a bus instead of owning a car, live with roommates or your parents instead of alone, don't take vacations or eat out, work more hours and spend less time with friends, have an old cell phone instead of a new one, buy second-hand clothes at a thrift shop instead of new ones), but each of these decisions is still a choice, which means that saving is a choice.

In the end, it doesn't really matter why people don't save. Things go wrong in life, and you need a big margin of error. Saving money is not optional if you're serious about building wealth and reducing the financial stress in your life.

Save money by cutting small expenses

Saving money doesn't have to be done in million-dollar chunks. A few dollars here and a few dollars here, given sufficient time and compound growth, can grow to be quite significant.

For example, if you can find a way to cut $25 per month from your cable or streaming bills, chances are you'd still be left with more entertainment than you could watch in a lifetime. If you save that money and invest it in a broad selection of stocks, you should be able to generate 7% per year. After a 40-year career, you'd have $65,620 added to your net worth.

Maybe you could switch from a $4 Starbucks coffee every morning to the free coffee in the office (the coffee in the office might taste like battery acid, but considering that I hate coffee, this one is easy for me). Over the course of a year, you'd save $1,000 just on coffee. Not only that, you'd save $1,000 after taxes, which is like getting a $1,500 pre-tax bonus. Would you be willing to drink office coffee for a year in exchange for a $1,500 bonus? After 40 years, the coffee savings would grow to $199,635, and as an extra bonus, you would learn to appreciate battery acid!

Perhaps you could find an apartment that's $100 per month cheaper than where you currently live. If you live there for five years before you upgrade to a nicer place, your retirement funds would grow by $76,436. You might also consider getting a roommate when you're starting out or finding some other way to cut your housing cost by more than $100 per month. The more you save, the wealthier you'll be in the long run.

You don't have to cut specifically cable, coffee, and apartment amenities to save for the long run, but you should cut somewhere. No savings is too small; small savings become giant sums of money given enough time and enough compound growth.

Save money by cutting large expenses

The two biggest financial vampires that feast off your ability to save are housing and transportation. That's not an accident. Banks fall over themselves to lend money to people for cars and houses. The loans are backed by assets and are not particularly risky for banks, especially when they can sell the loans to investors.

Individuals also love borrowing money to spend on stuff they can show off to other people, and the more money people borrow for showing off, the happier they feel at the time of the purchase. When you combine that instinct with a generous bank, the results are disastrous.

Consider a car. If a typical new car costs $40,000, but a reliable and unexciting used car costs $5,000, the used car would save you $35,000. You'd obviously have to pay more for repairs, so let's say you'd save only $25,000 after a few years of fixing up the old car. Over 40 years at 7%, that one decision to by a cheap used car instead of a shiny new car would add $374,361 to your net worth.

It's doubtful a new car could ever be worth the cost. When you enter your retirement years, would you say to yourself, "My net worth is $374,000 lower, but at least I got to have a new car 40 years ago"? Somehow, I don't think so.

Housing can have a similarly large impact. If you're looking to buy a house for $400,000, perhaps you might consider something a little smaller or a little older that costs $350,000. On a 30-year mortgage at 3%, the difference in your monthly payment would be only $211, so it doesn't seem like it matters at first. But if you invest that $211 savings each month and earn 7% on it, over 40 years you'll have an extra $505,897.

The slightly cheaper house and the used car together add almost $900,000 to your net worth in retirement. The younger you are when you start cutting costs and the bigger the savings, the larger the impact when you get older. Major expense changes like this might require some compromises and creativity, and you won't get the same joy that comes from boasting to other people about the expensive things you bought, but the long-term payoff is extraordinary.

Refocus your targeted spending levels

A major area of financial confusion for many people is capital vs. income. On the surface, money is money, and if you have money, you can spend it. But not all money should be treated the same way.

Income is money you can reasonably expect to recur on a regular basis. It could be a regular paycheck, or dividends, or a draw from your business. It's anything where, if you spend it now, you can be pretty sure you'll be getting more later. You should almost always plan your budget and your spending in the context of how much income you have, since you can't hurt yourself too badly spending something you'll get more of later.

Capital, by contrast, is money that isn't going to come back again. It's one-off money. It can take the form of money you have in the bank or money you have invested, and which, if spent, is gone forever. Your capital is your lifeline for the future; it's the source of your financial security, your job and retirement choices, and, important for many people, it's the source of the settlement you'll pay out to your spouse when you get divorced.

The only time you'd want to spend your capital, to waste it utterly and completely until there's nothing left, is in the case of a divorce since you don't want your obnoxious and intolerable spouse to get any of it, especially after that thing that happened in Bermuda (although you should consult first with a divorce lawyer before you waste marital assets, preferably a divorce lawyer who wasn't in Bermuda at the time of the thing).

Capital also can come in the form of cash inflow. You might get a large, one-time bonus at work, or you might win the lottery, or you might get an inheritance from your long-lost great-aunt Berget in Belgium. Newly-received capital should never be spent; it should only be invested so that it can generate income for you in the future.

Imagine you receive a large inheritance. If you spend the money, you'll have a lot of fun now, but when it runs out, there won't be another inheritance to replace it. Most people aren't in the habit of dying twice. The spending option will lead to a lifestyle spike and a lifestyle crash, or worse yet, it'll lead to an unaffordable lifestyle that you try to keep afloat by taking on debt. On the other hand, if you invest the inheritance, you'll receive investment income year after year forever, and you can safely spend that income, year after year, without it ever running out. You'll have a smaller spike in your lifestyle, but you'll never crash either.

Investing capital can also mean paying down debt. The rate of return you receive on debt payments is equal to the interest rate on the debt. For example, if you pay off a credit card at 28% interest, you're getting a 28% return on investment by paying off your credit card. If you pay off a mortgage at 3%, you're getting a 3% return on investment. Paying down debt and investing for income both have the effect of improving your long-term standard of living, more so than anything you could spend the money on.

While you're adjusting your spending levels to rely entirely on income, it's a good idea to avoid spending income you haven't received yet. There are all sorts of products, cars in particular, that make it possible to buy something with easy monthly payments. People are in the habit of making purchases based on what monthly payment fits into their monthly income budget.

That's certainly better than consuming capital for your monthly payments, but it's the wrong way to look at purchases. That new cell phone might cost only $30 per month, which you can afford easily, but if it's paid over 36 months, you're coughing up nearly $1,100 for the cell phone. If you would never dream of spending $1,100 for a cell phone, why would you consider spending $30 per month for 36 months? And yet people happily go with the monthly-payment option all the time.

Instead, consider whether the one-time price of $1,100 for the cell phone makes sense based on your budget. If you can afford it while funding all your other priorities, it's okay to spend a lot if you want to. If spending $1,100 would hurt your ability to fund other priorities, then it doesn't matter how small the monthly payment is. You should buy something cheaper.

The excessive focus on monthly payments is called "payment shopping," and retailers know full well that it's easier to sell expensive things as a stream of small payments than it is to sell it as a single, large payment, mostly because people are bad at math and don't know what they're really spending. Unless you want to hurt yourself financially and give in to retail psychological tricks, just ignore the monthly-payment numbers.

But it's fun to spend money NOW!

The compounding power of financial growth over long periods of time is easy to calculate, but the benefit is off in the distant future, a time so far away that it seems it'll never come. On the other hand, spending money now is something you can do now, and that's lots of fun! How can you change your mindset to make spending less fun?

In the movie Brewster's Millions, Montgomery Brewster stood to inherit $300 million from a long-lost great uncle, but the will required him to consume $30 million in one month. The idea is to teach Montgomery how to hate spending money so he'll be careful with his inheritance. The movie is a comedy which shows that spending money, even when you're trying to waste it, is as hard as earning it. After heroic efforts and some setbacks involving accidentally earning more money, Brewster meets the challenge, inherits the fortune, and never again wants to spend money.

It's impractical for most people to curb their spending impulses by spending $30 million in one month, and even if you had that much money lying around, it would probably be inadvisable to waste it all trying to change your habits. But there are some ways you can approach spending to give yourself pause.

<u>Consider the old adage: Time is money</u>. As far as old adages go, this one is older than most, and although it is rooted in truth and wisdom,

"older than most" is not seen as a great selling point in adages any more than it would be for an "older than most" cold-cut-combo sandwich at Subway. But if you look past the horror of an ancient sandwich, there's an incredibly useful tool here.

What does it mean to work for wages? You sell your time in exchange for money. You lose 40 hours a week plus commuting and stress, and you gain money (from which the government helps itself to a generous portion for taxes). The money you earn doesn't just fall from the sky; you lost part of your life in order to get it.

Maybe you would have wasted the time anyway watching TV or enjoying your hobbies (personally, I find my hobbies to be a great use of time, but my wife disagrees and would probably prefer that I spend my time earning money to help her pursue her hobbies which aren't a waste of time, unlike mine), but the point remains that you gave up something in order to get the money. If you turn around and waste the money on something like credit card interest or a lucite-encased slice of pepperoni pizza, you're really wasting your time.

You can even figure out how much time you're wasting. If you earn $20 per hour after taxes, and the preserved pepperoni pizza piece costs $50, then you just wasted 2 ½ hours. You might not think anything of spending $50, but would you want to spend 2 ½ hours working at a job you might hate in order to get a trinket?

What if you spent $220 on credit card interest for the month? That works out to 11 hours of your time. $220 might not seem like a big deal, but is it worth spending 11 hours per month simply to pay interest on money you borrowed because you wanted to buy stuff months ago instead of waiting until you had cash on hand to pay for it?

What about a small thing like a $5 coffee? That's 15 minutes of your life, which is a lot of time to lose for a cup of coffee. What about a $5,000 vacation? That's 250 hours, or over six weeks of full-time labor. How would it make you feel to work for 6 weeks in order to pay for one week of vacation? Probably you'd feel pretty bad.

And that's the goal. Just as Montgomery Brewster learned to hate spending money, calculating just how much of your life is going to waste on each purchase can help you to learn how to hate spending as well.

As an aside, when you reach the point of retirement, this mindset helps to make the transition process easier. You're not losing your income, which can seem scary to many people; instead, you're deciding to enjoy your time instead of selling it. You just stopped making the trade of time for money. There's no loss involved.

<u>Marry a woman who complains incessantly that any amount of money you spend is too much, no matter how much you have</u>. Admittedly, this tip doesn't work for everyone, but if you have a spouse who badgers you about spending, any joy you might get from making a purchase gets destroyed in the process of hearing all the complaining about it. Someone who can help you to stop enjoying life can help you to save money since you won't want anything anymore. A spouse like this can also help you make sure your money lasts the rest of your life since you won't want to live very long.

<u>Out of sight, out of mind</u>. Oscar Wilde said, "I can resist anything except temptation." If you find yourself in this category, at least where money is concerned, your best option for not spending is by not having money.

Obviously, bankrupt people don't spend as much as non-bankrupt people, but since your goal is financial success instead of financial failure (unless you're divorcing the spouse who badgers you constantly about spending and who takes all the joy out of life, in which case you want to look like a failure for the divorce court), you need to make yourself feel like you're bankrupt without actually being bankrupt.

The easiest way to do to that is to hide money from yourself.

If you have a 401(k) plan at work, you should direct part of your paycheck directly into that plan. If you have the option for multiple direct deposits, you should deposit some of your paycheck into a separate account that you never use for spending. If you can set up automatic transfers at your bank, you should have some money automatically transferred from your regular spending account into another account for saving or investing.

The idea here is that you want your money to be put away before you have a chance to see it waiting to be spent. There are many different ways to go about this, and it doesn't matter which one you choose. As long as you put your money somewhere that is less accessible to you, you increase the difficulty of accessing it, and you reduce the odds that you'll spend it.

The other side of savings: income

Not spending money is one way to increase your savings rate, but you can also increase your savings rate by earning more.

For the vast majority of people, the biggest asset they have is their time, which they sell for money at a job. If you're starting out a 40-year career that averages $50,000 per year of income (not counting taxes, investment growth, inflation, etc.), you're looking at $2 million that you have available to you. Obviously, you have to use much of this in order to live, but it still leaves a large amount of money to dedicate to other priorities.

What happens, then, if you find a way to increase your income from $50,000 to $60,000 per year? Over 40 years, that's an additional $400,000, which can fix an awful lot of financial problems.

Increasing your income is easier said than done, but generally the best way to approach that is by investing in yourself. Find ways to improve your skill set and add more value at work. That might mean coming up with a creative way to do something better than you're doing it, or it might mean taking additional training and obtaining certifications. Many employers recognize the value of employees who improve productivity and reduce costs, and that recognition often turns into pay increases.

If you're in a situation where your employer is too obtuse to recognize that you're driving improvements to his bottom line, and if your pay rate won't budge, then you might have to consider another job. One person I know worked as a car salesman and earned a commission on every car he sold. He was a great salesman, and he sold vastly more cars than anyone else at his dealership, bringing great success to the owner and a high income for himself. Because he was so successful, the owner fired him for being too expensive.

That was obviously a stupid move on the part of the owner, but stupid employers are as much a part of reality as stupid employees. If you find yourself in that position, it doesn't mean you're doing anything wrong by investing in your own skillset and creativity to enhance value. It just means you have to create value for someone else where the recognition and money will follow.

It might turn out that the best employer to work for is yourself. You might find some way to turn your skills into a side business or consulting operation. Those are great options to do full time, but side businesses can also work well as a supplement to a full-time job. You might find there's a way to invest some of your capital into your business to grow it faster, or you might prefer to invest some of your capital as a way to generate dividend income.

Options for generating more income are quite broad and are heavily dependent on what you like to do, what you're able to do, and your circumstances. It doesn't matter what you choose; earning more money will add directly to your savings rate.

One point to consider, however, if you're trying to decide between cutting expenses vs. earning more money, is that cutting expenses is generally the better option. Generating additional income consumes your time, and the government helps itself to a generous portion of whatever you produce. If you cut expenses, you keep your time and there are no taxes at all. Ideally, however, you should do both.

How much to save

Although there's no magic answer for a correct savings rate for everyone, as a rule of thumb you should aspire to save 20% of your take-home pay. If you invest everything you save, you'll be able to replace your income from work within about 35 years, and you'll have significantly higher income if you can keep working and saving a full 40 years.

Depending on your exact investment returns, you might be able to retire a few years earlier or a few years later, but a 20% savings rate gets you to where you need to be within the length of a normal career. With savings of 20% per year, over 40 years, and with a 7% after-inflation investment return, you'll have 40 times your income saved up. That'll be enough money to generate retirement income of 160% of your salary automatically and forever.

For example, a person who earns $40,000 per year and who saves 20% starting at age 25 will have accumulated $1.6 million by age 65. A portfolio of that size can generate $64,000 of annual income. That's twice as much income as this person would have been used to spending each year since he would have been living on only 80% of his income the whole time, and it's probably more money than he needs.

That's part of the goal too: giving yourself a margin of error. What if you can work only 30 years instead of 40? What if your investments generate only 6% instead of 7%? What if your savings rate drops below 20% from time to time? If any of those things happen, you'll probably be okay if you start with a high-enough savings rate.

While saving 20% seems like an ambitious goal for most people, it's not impossible, especially if you begin early in your career. You should start off by saving whatever you can. Even if it's only $10 a week, it'll be more than $0. Over time, as you earn raises or find ways to increase your income, you should save 100% of the raise and continue to live within your old budget.

The most difficult element of that plan is avoiding lifestyle creep. People have a tendency when they earn more money to spend more upgrading their lifestyle, which is followed by more upgrades in future years as income increases further, thus creating a cycle where it's never possible to save anything.

If you increase your income even 5% per year and you hold your lifestyle constant for four years, at the end of the four years you'll be at a 20% savings rate. Once you've achieved the 20% savings rate, you'll be in a position to spend all future raises upgrading your lifestyle to your heart's content for the rest of your career. The key is simply trying to hold the line while you get started in the process.

If you do spend a few years without lifestyle upgrades, you might find that you become used to that lifestyle and you might not automatically spend future raises. You might even end up with a savings rate that goes way beyond 20%.

Your savings rate is more important than your investment return

As you accumulate money and begin investing, it's tempting to wonder if you have your investment allocation right, or if you're investing correctly in the most exciting and dynamic things that'll revolutionize the future and make you rich overnight.

The answer is that it really doesn't matter. You'll make investment decisions as well as you can, and they'll probably end up fine over the long run, but your investment rate of return is really not that important compared to your savings rate, especially when you're starting out.

If you're saving $10,000 per year, after your first five years you'll have $57,500 accumulated at 7% per year. If your investments do really badly and generate only 2% per year, you'll still have $52,000 accumulated. But if you save only $8,000 per year instead of $10,000, even with a really good 10% investment return you'll have only $48,800 after five years. Higher savings are more important than higher returns.

Your investment returns matter more when you're older, but your savings rate early on is the thing that gets you to where you need to be. This is actually wonderful: Your savings rate is something you directly control, but you can't control your investment return. Being in charge of the most important part of your long-term wealth creation means that you don't have to be a great investor to do well, you just have to save enough.

The more you save, the less of a return you have to earn on your investments to reach your long-term wealth goals.

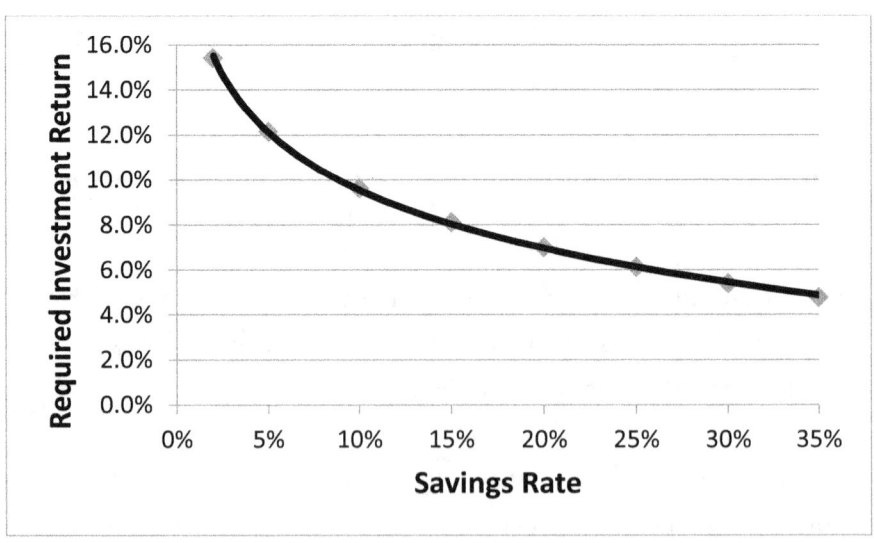

Over a 40-year career with a 20% savings rate, your investments need to generate a 7% return to grow enough to support a retirement income of 160% of your annual salary. If you save 30%, you need only 5.4% return per year. But if you save only 2% per year, you'll need a staggering 15.4% annual investment return, an average rate of return so high that only members of Congress are able to achieve it.

The same relationship applies between your savings rate and the number of years you need to work before you can retire. With the same long-term goal, but this time fixing the investment return at 7%, here's how many years you'd have to save before you can stop working:

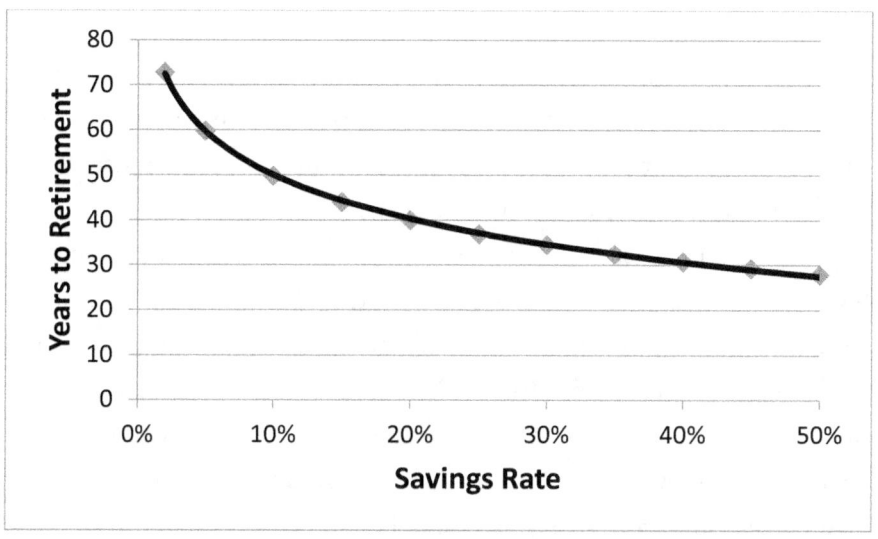

A 20% savings rate allows you to retire in 40 years, which is a pretty common goal. A 50% savings rate gets you down to 28 years, and a 2% savings rate requires 73 years of working and saving before you can call it quits.

Now, there are a lot of things you can change in these graphs. For example, you could set a different goal or a different margin of error. You could calculate how much you need to save to replace your annual expenses rather than your annual income. You might tinker with the investment-return assumptions. Or you might consider that after working a 73-year career, your retirement probably won't be that long and you won't need much money.

Whatever your base assumptions, the relationships between savings rate, required investment return, and years of working are all the same. A *higher* savings rate *reduces* the number of years you have to work and it *reduces* your required investment return. A *lower* savings rate *increases* the number of years you have to work and it *increases* your required investment return. The lower savings rate doesn't just increase the difficulty of achieving retirement goals; it increases the difficulty dramatically.

Once you've gotten yourself into a position of saving money, you have to remember that whatever you save is capital; this is money for your future and not for consumption, and the only appropriate use of the money is for things that generate returns.

Broadly speaking, you'll want to use savings for paying off high-rate debt and extinguishing other debts, building a cash emergency fund, contributing to your retirement accounts, and investing in a diversified portfolio of stocks. You could even invest savings in a business or other profit-making venture. But whatever you do, don't spend the money. Don't look at your accumulated wealth and decide to run out and spend it all on a rare collection of anime figurines, even if the collection is one-of-a-kind and discounted 40% compared to the book value. The capital you accumulate for your future is there to provide income for your future, not for buying junk now.

CHAPTER 11:
CARS

I am not a car person. I don't appreciate design or style, I don't care about engines, I don't need the latest tech, and I have no idea why someone who isn't a construction worker would ever need a pickup truck. I'm not interested in what people think about my car, shiny paint does nothing for me, and I hate new-car smell. Seeing a car in a commercial makes me think only about why I'm even watching a commercial.

My Dad bought a Mercury Grand Marquis many years ago, and he kept it until my Mom told him to get rid of it because it was too old and it was embarrassing. So he gave it to me and it became my first car. I kept the car until it was over twenty years old and rusting, and the only reason I got rid of it was because it stopped running and my wife said not to fix it since it embarrassed her.

My second car was a used Mercury Grand Marquis that I bought myself. I kept that car until it was over twenty years old, at which point it was no longer able to run in reverse and both my wife and my mother said it was embarrassing and I should get rid of it.

Then I bought a used Toyota – it was the newest car I ever owned at only eight years old, and I still drive it today.

I am in the minority of the population. I don't care about cars, so saving money on cars comes easily to me. Unfortunately, most people approach car buying as a way to commit financial suicide. Cars are the second biggest expense for most people, after housing, and for people who aren't suicidal, this is one of the most fruitful areas of your financial life to improve.

Why do people like destroying themselves for a machine?

People are really bad at planning for the future. People are really bad at understanding financing. Banks understand financing and love making low-risk loans on secured assets, while people love borrowing money to buy expensive stuff. When you put it all together, you get disastrously-high car debt.

But the financial confusion explains only part of the picture. There are other wasteful ways to go into debt, but cars are by far the most common for two reasons. The first is that cars have a certain level of utility to them, which is to say they serve the purpose of helping you to get around and to get to a job, which is a very strong justification for the purchase. Once you establish that you "need" a car, the line between needs and wants in car features gets blurred pretty badly. The other reason is that cars also have an artistic value which serves as a status symbol.

There's nothing more fun than feeling important and successful, and showing people how much money you can spend on art proves that you're successful enough to waste your money. The giant "M" sign at a McDonald's restaurant doesn't do anything useful; it's just there to show everyone that the restaurant has so much quality invested in its food that it can also waste money on a giant letter. The BMW logo on your car doesn't make the car better; it just shows everyone you earned enough money to stick an expensive logo on the front of your car. And when you're stuck in traffic, your car can't go any faster than the minivan in front of you, even if your car is shiny and sleek, but at least the other people on the road can see how much money you spent for artistic style.

When you step back to think about it, how much money do you really want to spend on art? Is your art budget really the most important priority you have? Do you really want to take on debt so you can impress your neighbors, friends, coworkers, dates, and strangers in parking lots with your amazing status of wasting money on style? Even if you do want to spend money on status seeking, you shouldn't unless the date you're trying to impress is really good looking. Worse yet, if the car helps you to get things to work out with your date, you could end up with someone who is interested in destroying wealth, not building it.

The tragedy of the whole thing is that showing off your wealth by destroying it conspicuously on something like a car is socially acceptable, but if you were to run around showing strangers in a parking lot how much money you saved in your 401(k), you would be considered a social pariah akin to someone walking around with his finger in his nose.

Why is this? I don't know. There is probably someone who spent $400,000 on social science degrees who could try to answer that question, but it really doesn't matter. Overcoming social biases is just one of those things you have to do if you want to succeed in the long run.

How you should purchase cars

The answer is simple: stick with an inexpensive, used car that helps you to get around, even if it's old and not fancy. You don't have to take it to my extreme of driving a 20-year-old piece of junk that's rusted and that doesn't go in reverse (which makes for an interesting experience in parking lots) and which embarrasses your wife, but you should definitely avoid anything related to seeking status.

That, of course, begs the question of how you know whether or not a car feature has utility to make your life better, or whether it's just a status item. The test is quite simple: When you look at the feature, do you think first about how it will help you, or do you think first about how other people will react?

Power windows, for example, have great utility. They make it easier to get fast-food orders and to spit without making a disgusting mess to clean up later, but nobody buys power windows thinking about how impressed everyone else will be. But when it comes to buying a Porsche, does anyone buy one for reasons other than impressing people? Probably not.

Where to draw the line isn't the same for everyone, but as long as you're aware that there is a line and that you should draw it somewhere, you're ahead of the game regardless of where you draw it.

Similarly, you should buy used instead of new. A used car doesn't impress anyone, but it's a lot cheaper. Many people make the mistake of thinking a new car is a better value because it has a warranty and the repair costs are less. Those are certainly valuable features in favor of a new car, and avoiding a $3,000 surprise car-repair bill is great.

But how in the world does it make sense to pay $800 per month as a car payment, every single month for years, in order to avoid the chance of a costly repair bill? It doesn't. The only thing you get from that massive payment is a chance to watch your new car rapidly lose value as it becomes a used car. Buying used might result in more repair expenses, but what you save on monthly payments and depreciation more than covers any repair costs.

Many years ago when my first car was only 18 years old, the transmission failed. The mechanic told me it would cost $2,000 to repair at a time when the car was worth only $500. Rather than replacing the car, I paid for the new transmission. My goal wasn't to improve the resale value of my $500 car, but rather to keep it running longer so I wouldn't have to buy another car for a while. The car kept going for another two years before the engine died, at which point it became a total loss. But what I gained from the $2,000 expense was the use of a car for two years at an average cost of less than $100 per month. Even if I replaced my car with a cheap used car, it wouldn't have made as much financial sense as the repair since the other used car might have had its own mechanical issues. At least with my own car, I knew in advance what the other issues were.

There are limits, of course. Sometimes it makes sense to replace a used car with another used car rather than to keep operating a pile of rusty debris for the rest of eternity. The general rule of thumb I recommend is that if you can operate your car without your wife hiding her head in shame, and if you can get the car out of the driveway without having to put it in neutral and roll down a hill, you should keep the old car, pay for repairs, and save the monthly payment.

I make the point about the savings in the form of a monthly payment to make it more relatable, but payments are another area where people get themselves tripped up.

A car might cost $300 per month or $700 per month or whatever you can afford out of your budget each month, and if you're making a budget, that's at least a great start. But how long do those payments last? If you're paying every month for 36 months, that's a lot different than paying for 84 months. Most people never bother to add up the total of all the payments to see what the car actually costs as long as they know the payment is affordable.

The car dealer doesn't have any incentive to help you with that process either. His goal is to make the car seem as cheap as possible so he can make his sale and get his commission, and the easiest way to do that is to spread out the car loan over more months, or worse, to persuade you to lease instead of buy, which is cheaper monthly, but which doesn't even leave you with a car at the end of the term.

People focus on the monthly payments almost exclusively, and this trap is so easy to fall into that the nefarious car dealer will twist the ends of his waxed mustache and laugh maniacally as soon as he closes the sale (or so I've been told; my source on the maniacal laughing is my seven-year-old daughter, and as much as I love her, I have to admit that her reporting on the nature of the world isn't always the most accurate).

Similarly, car dealers might advertise 0% financing, or no payments for 90 days, or cash back, or other great ways that allow you to get the car now and to worry about paying for it later. If you get bargain financing, that's wonderful, but you have to remember you're buying a machine and not a financial instrument.

It doesn't matter how great the financing terms are; you should never let the financing influence how much money you spend. Instead, decide how many total dollars you want to commit to the car purchase, and if you need to finance it, only then should you seek out the best financing deal.

The best financing option, for two reasons, is to pay cash for the car. The first reason is that using cash forces you to be mindful of the total cost of your purchase. Writing a large check focuses you in a way that is lost in a loan agreement, and it imposes discipline on you not to exceed your budget. The second reason is that having cash protects you from the cost of external financing.

One person I know really wanted to get a new car, but he had bad credit. However, he found a car dealer who would make him a loan at an affordable monthly payment; all it required was 26.9% interest, which is almost as bad as the worst possible credit card interest.

Another person I know bought a car and the helpful dealer figured out monthly payments for her. She knew the total price of her car and the payment, but she didn't know how to calculate the interest rate. I calculated it for her: 15%. That's not as bad as 26.9%, but you'll almost never find an investment opportunity that returns 15%, and it's a tragic waste to give that kind of a return to someone else (fortunately this person paid back the loan right away).

Even the 0% advertised rates often aren't really 0%. If a car costs $30,000, and it comes with a choice of 0% financing or $2,000 cash back, then the 0% financing is a fraud.

The cash cost of the car is really $28,000 if you pay cash ($30,000 less the cash back), but if you finance it, you're effectively paying $28,000 for the car plus $2,000 in interest to get up to the $30,000 total. On a 5-year loan, that works out to 2.3% per year. That's not a bad rate, but it's certainly not 0%.

It baffles me how it's even legal to advertise a loan this way. I suspect the mustache-twirling-car-dealer association must have lobbied Congress to be allowed to commit accounting and loan fraud, but it's also possible that some influential legislator somewhere got a really good car deal and wanted to make sure everyone else could get in on the action.

Unless you know how to calculate the actual interest rate on financing that involves giving up a cash back option, you're probably better off sticking with a cash payment option.

But whatever you do, remember that a car is a black hole for money, and try to keep the expense as small as possible.

CHAPTER 12: HOUSING

Along with transportation, housing is the other major area where people waste money like a drunk Congressman (okay, maybe I exaggerate a bit here; you'd have to buy 100,000 houses at $1 million each and burn them to the ground to get anywhere close to the level of waste Congress manages to achieve). But even without Congressional excess, people hurt themselves on housing.

The primary influence here is the same as with cars: People want to feel important and to get validation from others about how successful they are, and while they can't do this by yelling to passersby about how much money they have invested, they can do this by making a big show of spending all their money on a house.

The secondary influence is external pressure: The home seller, of course, wants you to spend a much as you can since he's the direct recipient of your money; your friends and family want you to spend as much money as you can on a house so they can justify to themselves that overspending on their houses was a grand idea; your realtor wants you to spend as much as you can to maximize his commission; your mortgage broker wants you to spend as much as you can to maximize his commission; your banker wants you to spend as much as you can to maximize the profit for the bank when they package and sell your loan to someone else; the government wants you to spend as much as you can to maximize the tax base; the neighbors want you to spend as much as you can to maximize the value of their homes.

The pressure to spend is enormous and it comes at you from all directions. The pressure to save money comes only from within, quiet, invisible, and without a single person applauding you for your thrift.

Maybe, if you're lucky, your spouse will applaud your thrift, but you're just as likely to get complaints about not buying nice enough presents for that anniversary you forgot for the second year in a row, and the only way to make up for that is with an extra bathroom and a renovated kitchen. You're basically on your own. You have to decide for yourself that it's important to prioritize planning for your financial future by cutting your housing expense, and you're going to feel like everyone is against you, but this is important.

How to cut your housing expenses

There are limits on how far you can cut your housing expenses. The obvious extreme, of course, is to be homeless, but that option isn't very popular. Not only does my wife not wish to be homeless, but even before I was married, I agreed it was better to have a little less money and instead enjoy a working bathroom that wasn't at a bus stop.

Even without extremes, it is possible to spend less on housing, especially when starting out.

When you're fresh out of college, that's an excellent time to live with your family for a little while longer to keep your expenses down. Or you might decide that you prefer to be on your own, but you're willing to split the cost of housing by having a roommate. You might also decide that after your roommate abandons his responsibility for his part of the lease because he doesn't feel happy enough at the house, you need to sue him in the local district court, submit the case to the Judge Judy TV show, and ultimately settle for about half of what he owed you because that was as much money as he had and he was too foolish to accept the Judge Judy offer to appear on the show and have them pay his judgement while also providing a free trip to California for you and a "witness" of your choice (just to pick a hypothetical example not based on a former roommate of mine by the name of D. Morick, or perhaps Dan M. to protect his identity better, and who, by the way, still should pay that last $1,000 he owes me even though I agreed I wouldn't pursue it).

You might also decide to save money by living in a smaller apartment rather than a larger one, or one that's a little farther away from where you want to be, or one that has some other compromise. Perhaps you'd want to save money by living with mice, or by bartering housekeeping services for room and board, which worked great for both Cinderella and Snow White respectively, at least according to my little daughter.

There are many tradeoffs you can make to keep costs down, and there are a few important things to keep in mind while considering what you need vs. what you want.

First, don't pick a house or apartment with the expectation of impressing other people. As soon as you spend your money to make other people think you're great, you've lost. Second, don't pick a place to live based on having room for guests. If you have your heart set on having people visit you, it's almost always cheaper to pay for guests' hotel bills than it is to pay for extra bedrooms that sit vacant most of the time.

Third, don't pick a place based on how wonderful it'll be for entertaining. The "entertainment" functions of a house are costly, and if you have more parties to justify the extra housing expense, you'll also have more party expenses, which might be fun if you like parties (which I hate), but which also drains resources from your future.

Remember that there's no shame in having a modest lifestyle.

My wife and I lived in apartments for seven years before we bought a house to accommodate our growing family, and we didn't feel at all deprived, but we did enjoy saving more money during that period.

If you're concerned that your friends will think less of you because of the housing choices you make for yourself, you should consider getting new friends. There's already enough pressure in life to spend money without also spending time around people who want to make the pressure worse. Once you get to later stages in life, you'll find it's easier to get more friends than it is to get more money, so you'd best plan in advance.

Whatever you choose to do to keep your housing cost below what you can afford to pay, make sure that you save the extra money rather than spending it on other stuff you don't need. Giving up something you want in housing only to waste the money on something else is counterproductive.

Buy or rent?

When you decide on your preferred housing, you have to face the second-oldest question out there: Should I buy or rent? The oldest question is "Are you sure it's a good idea to eat this apple, Eve?" The good news is that if you make a wrong decision here, you don't have to worry about wrecking the future of humanity, unlike with the apple question (coincidentally, the apple question also involved buying or renting, specifically whether to continue renting in the Garden of Eden, admittedly at a very good rate, or whether to strike out into the world as an independent owner).

Unlike much of personal finance, the question of whether to buy or rent can be solved with 100% mathematical certainty. All you have to do is answer a few simple questions:

1. How long are you going to stay in the house?

2. How long are you going to stay in your current job?
3. How much is your income going to change over time?
4. What are interest rates going to be when you move out in the future?
5. How much are rental rates going to increase over time?

6. How much are property taxes going to increase? Note: property taxes never decrease.
7. How much is the home going to appreciate or depreciate?
8. How much are you going to spend on repairs and maintenance?
9. What is the opportunity cost of investments you could have made with your down payment?
10. How long is your marriage going to last?

11. How many years will it be before your wife gets tired of wherever you're living and starts complaining incessantly that she hates the place and can't be happy until you move somewhere better?
12. Is your family always going to be the same size?
13. Are the local schools always going to be satisfactory?

These questions are somewhat difficult to answer as they require knowledge of the future, and unless you have access to a time machine (and if you do, it begs the question of why you're wasting your time thinking about how to pay for your house), the answers to these questions are unknowable. Thus, the mathematical calculation is impossible and you don't have to agonize over making a wrong decision.

There are, fortunately, some guides and rules of thumb to point you in a direction that's more likely to be right than wrong.

<u>Do you have at least a 20% down payment?</u> If not, keep renting. This

isn't an unbreakable rule; people can and do buy houses with smaller down payments while still turning out okay. But if you have the down payment ready in advance, it shows three things: 1) you're able to save money and build capital over long periods of time, 2) you're self-disciplined and patient, and 3) you're able to plan ahead. All three of those traits are helpful in homeownership since it's a long-term proposition and one fraught with surprise expenses.

The larger down payment also reduces your housing costs since you can avoid private mortgage insurance premiums and qualify for lower interest rates. Paying increased financing costs to rush into a house before you've built up the down payment might be more fun since you get the house faster, but it's a real expense which is best avoided.

<u>Do you reasonably expect to stay in the same location for the next five to ten years?</u> If not, you should keep renting. Purchasing a home involves large numbers of closing costs for things like owner's title insurance, transfer taxes, inspections, mortgage fees, recording taxes, and so forth.

Selling a home involves large numbers of closing costs for things like realtor commissions, transfer taxes, recording taxes, and the like (note that the government happily taxes you on both the purchase and the sale, as well as your ownership in between; and what a great thing too! We wouldn't want the government to feel sad and left out of the transaction, or to miss out on the chance to share in your housing joy).

Over long periods of time, housing appreciation helps to offset these costs; over short periods of time, transaction costs can wipe you out. Time is your friend.

<u>Do you believe your income and your marriage are stable?</u> A failure in

either one could force you to sell sooner than you expect, which triggers all of the nasty transaction costs. Owning a home also reduces your mobility, which gives you fewer options if you need to make a job or spouse change.

<u>Can you handle surprise repair costs?</u> If you suddenly need to spend $2,000 to replace a leaking water heater or $10,000 for a new HVAC system, you need to have some reasonable plan to cope with the expense without resorting to high interest debt or raiding your retirement account.

You might get lucky and not have any major repairs for many years, but counting on luck isn't a plan.

If you answer "no" to any of these questions, you probably are not ready to buy. If you answer "yes" to every question, that doesn't automatically mean buying is the best option for you, but it is more likely to work in your favor than renting.

There are several other things you need to keep in mind. When you hear about how much you'll save on your taxes by owning a home, remember that the numbers are probably way overstated. Home ownership was once a good tax-saving tool, but with the changes in the Trump tax cut limiting state and local tax deductions, with the increase in the standard deduction, and with interest rates being very low, the tax savings are presently quite small.

When you estimate how much money you'll need for repairs, maintenance, and renovations, increase your budget by 50%. Costs are always higher than you think. A realistic number would be to budget to spend 1% of the home's value each year on repairs and maintenance. Ideally, you should set this budget aside into a savings account for easy access. If you save for a few years and suddenly have to pay $20,000 for roof repairs, it's a great feeling to have cash in the bank. If you don't have any repairs, you won't get hurt by having extra money.

It's good to remember as well that there's nothing inherently wrong with renting. You might hear that rent is just "throwing money away," but so is paying for mortgage interest, property taxes, and a replacement for that leaky water heater. Renting and buying both involve losing money in exchange for having a place to live, but you're simply losing money on different things. Buying a home might help you build equity as you pay off your mortgage and the home appreciates, but if you rent, you build equity by saving money and investing. Buying a home might help you to have a fixed mortgage payment, but renting has fewer surprise expenses (e.g., you don't have to pay for a new roof) and fewer costs if you decide to move. There's nothing morally flawed in renting a property.

Lastly, when making the decision to buy or rent, make sure you're comparing like properties. For example, if you presently rent an apartment and you're thinking of buying a house, the house is likely to be much more expensive because it's a much larger living space. If you actually need the space, the added cost might be worthwhile, but the added cost wouldn't have anything to do with the buying vs. renting decision. To get an idea of the real price difference, you should compare the cost to buy a house vs. renting a house, or the cost to buy a condo vs. renting an apartment.

Whatever decision you make in the end, the key is to make sure the decision is based on what works for you and not what works for everyone else. The realtors, bankers, and government all stick their fingers into the housing transaction and help themselves to little pieces. Your friends and family have their own opinions about what you should do. But you are the one who has to pay the bills in the end, and if the purchase doesn't make sense for you (people just starting out in life, for example, should almost always rent), then nobody else's opinion matters (except for your spouse's opinion, but only if your spouse is your wife; if your spouse is your husband, then it doesn't matter what he thinks because he's probably wrong anyway).

Home equity

You've probably heard about home equity. Banks might offer you a home-equity loan with easy payments to help you pay for needed repairs or that dream vacation you've always wanted (or that your spouse has always wanted, but which you'll go on anyway to stop the complaining). Other people talk about building equity through homeownership. So what exactly is home equity and how should you think about it in the context of your financial plans?

Your equity is the value of your house minus your debt on the house. The higher your equity, the higher your net worth, which is a great measure of your long-term financial success. In fact, if your house goes up in value enough, the government sends you a friendly congratulations in the form of a tax assessment notice, and to help you celebrate the increased value of your home, they also send you an increased property-tax bill.

So whence comes home equity? There are three components: 1) down payment, 2) declining mortgage balance, and 3) home appreciation.

The down payment is the most obvious source. If you buy a house for $400,000 with 20% down, you put up $80,000 in cash and borrow $320,000. The net value of your home, after subtracting all your debt from the value, is the $80,000 you put into it.

The declining mortgage balance is the next component. Your $320,000 debt isn't going to be $320,000 forever (unless you picked an interest-only mortgage or a negative-amortization mortgage that makes you poorer over time). A portion of every payment helps to reduce your remaining debt until it goes to $0 after 15 or 30 years.

At 3%, the $320,000 mortgage would have a payment of $1,349 per month for 30 years. For that first month, your debt goes down by

$549 and you pay $800 in interest. That means your remaining balance falls to $319,451, and your home equity rises to $80,549.

After making payments for 25 years, each new monthly payment reduces your mortgage balance by $1,158 and increases your equity by the same amount. With regular mortgage amortization, the principal portion of your payment increases, and your equity grows faster, which is a really neat feature.

The third way equity grows is through appreciation. If your $400,000 house goes up to $550,000 in ten years, you now have an additional $150,000 in equity.

When you put together the down payment, the principal payments, and the appreciation, the total is your home equity.

In this example, after ten years, the total home equity would be $80,000 (the down payment) + $77,343 (the principal portion of mortgage payments) + $150,000 (the appreciation on the home), for a total of $307,343. If you were to sell the home at that point, $307,343 is the amount of cash you'd have left over when you walk away and pay off your remaining mortgage balance.

Of course, this can go the other way too. During the housing boom, some people bought houses with 0% down, negative amortization loans that grew their debt, and which were then followed by declining home prices. Having everything go against you can result in negative equity, which means that if you sold the house, you'd have to write a giant check to the bank in order to give away your home.

That is a situation you desperately don't want since it can trap you in a house that might no longer be suitable for your needs, but fortunately that combination of problems is quite rare now. Most mortgages now require a down payment of some sort (20% is advisable to get the best rates, to avoid private mortgage insurance expenses (which are imposed on low-equity mortgages), and to develop a habit of saving), negative-amortization loans are almost non-existent, and more modest appreciation rates reduce the odds of having your house drop significantly in value in some future year.

While there is still a chance that your house might fall in value, the down payment and the regular mortgage payments help to cushion you from that risk. Drops in home values are also less likely the longer you own the home.

Now, once you've built up this nice, giant pile of equity, what do you do with it? If you listen to the banks and to your friends, you'll borrow against your equity to buy a new car or take vacation or remodel your kitchen, which is perfectly good already, but which for some reason is completely unusable unless you buy granite countertops, Brazilian cherry cabinets, and a $10,000 gourmet cooking range you'll never use because you are a lousy chef and you like restaurant food.

Your friends and the bank are all correct that you can borrow against your equity, but it doesn't answer the question of whether or not you should. The answer is you shouldn't.

Home equity serves as a store of wealth. You can borrow against it in case of emergency, you can use it to fund the purchase of a new house if you decide to move, and you can grow it to cover 100% of your home's value so that you can dump your monthly mortgage payment. Home equity could be a great way to free some capital to invest if you downsize during retirement. But as soon as you start to consume your wealth, you increase the financial risk in your life while remaining stuck in debt and reducing your options for the future.

That's something you should try to avoid.

Of course, there is an exception for every rule. I met a man in 2015 who spent all his time travelling, car racing, skydiving, drinking alcohol to excess, gambling, overeating, wasting money to impress people, and doing every dangerous and self-destructive thing he could think of. He said he chose that lifestyle because his doctor told him he had only two years to live. If you're pretty sure you're not going to have a future, then there's no need to save or plan for the future, and he probably got the decision right.

While a license for financial recklessness is perhaps one of the few side benefits of a very short lifespan, I can't say I recommend having a short lifespan as a financial strategy. Also, when I asked the man how long he lived this way, he said it was ever since he was diagnosed in 1984, so you might consider getting a second opinion before following his example.

Meanwhile, it's great when your home equity rises and your net worth goes up, but you don't want to let that trick you into spending more money than you otherwise would. You hurt yourself when you spend more.

You also don't want to buy a bigger house than you can afford simply for the opportunity to build more home equity. There is something called "house poor," when you have a high net worth, but it's all tied up in your house. Are you really wealthy if all of your cash flow goes toward mortgage payments, renovations, property taxes, and maintenance to such a degree that you can't enjoy your life by doing things you want?

The key in all this is buy a house priced lower than what you can afford and to look at the equity you accumulate as a future resource, but not one that's your primary focus.

CHAPTER 13:
INSURANCE

Insurance is critical to your financial success; insurance can also make it harder to achieve your goals.

This is a contradiction, just like many contradictions in life: wanting to balance work and family, but dedicating 75% of your effort to work and 10% to TV; complaining of boredom from your routine, and feeling uncomfortable whenever the routine changes; getting married and expecting to be happy.

But like many contradictions, insurance can fit into your life if you understand it..

Insurance is a way to manage risk. Some things in life are extremely expensive, like having your house burn down or breaking your leg while base jumping. You don't want to lose the money you worked hard to accumulate when one of those very expensive and unlikely events occurs, and by taking a small loss every month paying an insurance premium, an insurance company agrees to take the loss if something unexpected and expensive happens.

If the insurance is priced well, this is a good deal and it makes your finances much more predictable and much less susceptible to sudden destruction. The problem is that a lot of insurance is not priced well, and people purchase overpriced policies to insure tiny risks.

The pricing problem is easy to understand. When an insurance company decides how much to charge, it looks at the potential loss it could take (e.g., $300,000 when a house burns down) and the probability of that loss occurring (perhaps 0.03% per year). Multiplying those together gives the insurance company an expected annual loss of $90. But then they have to add in costs for management, secretaries, corporate offices, regulatory compliance, taxes, shareholder dividends, debt financing, customer acquisition, marketing, "business" travel to 5-star resorts, and all those annoying AFLAC duck commercials.

Suddenly that $90 expected loss becomes a $1,000 annual homeowner's insurance premium. This is true of all insurance: The premium is equal to expected losses plus overhead, and the more insurance you buy, the more overhead you pay for.

It's probably still worth it to pay $1,000 to make sure you never have to pay to rebuild your house if it's destroyed, but you're definitely paying more than the real risk you're offloading.

The other major problem people run into is insuring excessively-small risks. It's a shame to break or lose an $800 cell phone or to have a $200 microwave break down, but getting cell phone insurance or a microwave extended warranty to protect against a loss that you should be able to handle out of savings is just a waste of money. The individual premiums might be small, but over a lifetime they add up to tens of thousands of dollars, and the vast majority of that money is just going to insurance company overhead, not real risk reduction.

That's even assuming you reduce your risk. You may have noticed that insurance agreements are quite long, and the majority of the agreement lists all the reasons the insurance company doesn't have to pay you when things go wrong.

If you experience a loss and the insurance payout is quick and easy, that's great. If you have to engage an attorney or start litigation to get the payout you're entitled to, the value of your insurance just went way down based on the cost to collect. On big losses, it's worth the cost of litigating, but on small policies, like the cell phone or the microwave, litigating would be prohibitive, which would lead most people to give up. The insurance companies know that, and they don't make money by writing lots of checks.

When I bought my house, the previous owner included an appliance insurance policy. As luck would have it, my refrigerator started making strange, loud noises, and I called the appliance insurance company. They were kind enough to explain to me that because the refrigerator was still cold, it was therefore not broken, and they wouldn't cover the repairs. I tried to explain that a loud buzzing noise that keeps you awake at night is not an indicator of a properly-functioning appliance, but they still politely declined to pay.

If I had paid directly for this insurance, I would have been extremely annoyed, but since the old owner paid for it, I was only mildly annoyed.

The most bizarre warranty I ever came across was on a $5.00 clock at Kmart (which lets you know how long ago that was). The clock was warranted against all defects, and if it stopped working, all you had to do was ship it back to the factory at your own expense and enclose a check for $7.95 to cover return shipping. Why you would ever use the warranty instead of throwing away the clock and buying a new one is beyond me, and I can't figure out why the warranty even existed, but there it was. I ended up not buying the clock, so I didn't investigate further. Then Kmart went out of business, which is a lesson to all retailers who fail to have good warranties on their clocks.

Despite the overhead built into insurance premiums and the waste it generates, there are still times when you should purchase it:

1. If the potential loss is greater than you could afford to pay without damaging your finances,

2. If the premium is reasonable compared to the chance you

might experience a covered loss,

3. If the insurance is required by law (e.g., auto insurance) or a bank (e.g., homeowners insurance), and the insurance is cheaper than the fines or penalties for non-compliance,

4. If you're significantly riskier than the insurance company expects (e.g., your house is located next to a fireworks factory, you're 8 months pregnant, you have a toddler with a history of dropping your new cell phone into the toilet, or the local neighborhood kids enjoy an annual Halloween prank of burning down your house).

In all other circumstances, it's better to self-insure with your emergency fund as the backup funding source in case disaster strikes. You can be reasonably sure that at some point you'll have a loss that could have been covered had you purchased a specific insurance policy for that, but when you add up all the premiums you'll save over a lifetime, you can expect to come out way ahead with self-insurance.

Self-insurance can be a great way to improve your long-term finances, but it's a more advanced tool that's best left for a point in your life when you're already financially stable. If you buy a cell phone, most people could afford to self-insure the phone rather than paying extra each month on their cell-phone bill. If the cell phone is damaged or destroyed, buying a new phone probably won't ruin you. On the other hand, if you want to self-insure on something major like health insurance, you'd better have ample resources available to back you up in case you're hit with a major expense. The greater your wealth, the more you can self-insure, and the lower your wealth, the more insurance you should consider buying.

To the extent you can't self-insure a risk, such as your house burning to the ground, you can come up with a hybrid option through deductibles. The deductible is the portion of a covered loss you have to pay for before the insurance kicks in.

Insurance companies like deductibles because they mean a lower risk of small claims. In exchange for taking on the risk of small claims yourself, the insurance company gives you a discount on the premium to protect you on big claims, sometimes a very large discount.

For example, you might decide you want insurance on your home because a $300,000 loss in the case of fire would be insurmountable. If the house burns down and you have a $500 deductible, you would lose $500, and the insurance company would pay for the rest. If you have a $5,000 deductible, you would lose $5,000, and the insurance company would cover anything beyond that. The higher the deductible, the more risk you take and the less risk the insurer takes.

If a tree falls in your backyard and smashes your fence, you'd probably file a claim and have the insurance company pay if your deductible were only $500. But if your deductible were $5,000, you would probably just repair the fence yourself and leave the insurance out of it. Thus, a higher deductible means you're more likely to pay when small losses occur, and the insurance company is more likely to be off the hook. A higher deductible means you're self-insuring for more small losses.

The insurance companies don't give you any guidance on what the right deductible should be, except to tell you that the higher your deductible and the more responsibility you take for small losses, the lower your premiums. Since the goal is to minimize your insurance expense and the corporate overhead that bloats it, you want to pick the highest deductible you can afford to lose.

Maybe as a new homeowner who just put all your cash into a down payment, you could afford to lose only $500 if a tree lands on your garage. On the other hand, if you've been in the house a while and you have savings and equity, perhaps you could handle a $10,000 loss with no problem.

You pick a number that's high, maybe even a little higher than feels comfortable, but not so high that it would ruin you if you had to cover a loss that size. Over time, as you build your financial resources, you should steadily increase your deductibles on all your insurance policies so you can minimize your premium expenses.

While you make progress on reducing your reliance on outside insurance, there are a couple ways to track your self-insurance risks. One option is to calculate how much money you save on premiums every time you increase your deductible and put that money into a separate account. It could be a savings account or an investment account, but either way you'd have a separate fund available to you for managing risks and deductibles you choose not to insure. The separate account has the advantage of making your savings easy to see and manage, and the disadvantage of being another account to think about.

The other option is simply to recognize that your net worth is high enough to absorb a certain amount of risk and not to worry about the details. As long you don't spend the money you save by cutting your premiums and self-insuring your risks, it's not necessary to have a separate insurance account, but if you think you might be tempted to spend your savings, putting them into a separate account can help you to maintain your spending discipline.

As you ponder your insurance, it's important to understand the different types of insurance that exist, because you have to make a judgment about the relative costs and merits of each policy separately, what sorts of losses you expect, how much you can afford to lose, and what you're reasonably willing to pay to be protected from risk.

Auto insurance

Just about everyone needs auto insurance.

You could have a tree fall on your car, which might result in the need for a bit of touch-up work. Or you might be driving along, minding your own business, when a tiger escapes from your local zoo, dashes in front of you, and forces you to swerve into oncoming traffic, causing damage to your car, someone else's car, and assorted injuries to all involved, including the tiger.

Perhaps the tiger is driving another vehicle when he collides into you, and since he's a tiger, he has no money to pay the judgment against him after you win the lawsuit for his reckless, and probably unlicensed, driving.

It's bad enough to have to pay for repairs to your own vehicle, but surprise medical bills, legal defense costs, indigent or uninsured counterparties, and six-figure personal injury awards can very quickly damage the best-laid financial plans.

Insurance helps you to offload those risks, which, besides being potentially expensive, also are not all that rare (except for the tiger driving a car; that's quite rare). Auto insurance premiums are also reasonably priced relative to the risk you're offloading, which makes it a generally good value, in addition to falling into the "required by law" category.

Of course, auto insurance isn't a great value everywhere. In New Jersey, for example, premiums are extremely high for a few reasons. One is that New Jersey is a "no fault" state, meaning that the insurance company pays for accident damages even if you were dancing on the roof of your Tesla right before the crash or the other guy was switching seats with his pet tiger while the car was in motion.

If nobody is at fault in an accident, then everybody will file insurance claims for damages, no matter how trivial, and the cost of insurance rises regardless of how safe a driver you are.

New Jersey also mandates extremely generous medical benefits on auto insurance, thus incentivizing injured parties to seek as much medical care as possible, especially since they're not at fault.

Further, New Jersey limits the ability of insurance companies to charge higher premiums to riskier drivers. When you put this all together, the result is very high premiums for everyone, which then incentivizes people to take a chance driving uninsured, which creates uninsured motorist losses that drive up premiums even more.

New Jersey auto insurance isn't really insurance; it's a game of shuffling money around without regard to risk, which makes it a very poor tool if you're trying to limit your risk. It's not worth buying, except that it's required by law. But that's New Jersey, which has a lot of other problems too.

Whether you live in that horrible state or elsewhere, make sure to focus your insurance expense on protecting you against risk instead of serving as a prepaid expense.

Risk involves things like personal injury to yourself or others, major property damage, and legal defense costs, really big stuff that's uncommon and where the insurance can really save you from financial catastrophe. On the other hand, damage to your car is to be expected if you drive. Wear and tear and depreciation are facts of life, and so is the occasional fender bender. If you insure against a small expense that's likely to occur at some point, your insurance is just prepaying a future expense, not protecting you against risk, and that's not efficient.

There are two ways to minimize the prepaid expense component of your insurance. The first is to drive an inexpensive car so that damage to it isn't a big financial strain on you or the insurance company. You should be doing that anyway, but saving on your insurance premiums as a result is a bonus. The second is to drop collision coverage entirely and to take personal responsibility for damage to your own vehicle.

That might seem like a big risk, but you can cover repairs out of the money you save by avoiding collision coverage, and unless you're a riskier-than-average driver, you'll come out ahead on average. If you do need collision coverage because damage to your vehicle would be too costly, increase your deductible to the highest level you can afford to lose and consider switching to a less expensive car at some point in the future.

Similarly, you should increase your deductibles as high as you can for liability damage. If an accident costs you a few thousand dollars, you should be able to cover that from premium savings over many years. It's not fun paying a high deductible if there's an accident, but over long periods of time you'll come out ahead.

One exception: If you enjoy dancing on your car roof with your pet tiger while your car is in motion, or if you have a hobby of going out on Sundays to crash into other people, you might consider getting the lowest possible deductible. That's because you fall into the "riskier than the insurance company expects" category, and higher-than-expected risk is a case where you come out ahead with more insurance, not less.

While pricing your policy, you'll want to make sure your policy limits are as high as possible. The additional premiums for increasing coverage from $250,000 to $1 million isn't much, but if you have a severe accident causing you major injuries (or causing them to someone else), the difference between $250,000 and $1 million in benefits is huge and provides much more substantive protection. That's exactly the sort of thing insurance is supposed to do: charge you a small, periodic amount in premiums to protect you against a very large, unlikely risk.

Similarly, you must make sure you have uninsured motorist coverage. If you have an accident resulting in a serious injury and the other guy is at fault, there's no guarantee that the other guy will have the financial wherewithal to pay for what he's done, especially if he's a tiger. Winning a lawsuit and having a court order someone else to pay you for injuries does nothing if he's uninsured and broke. That is a very real and very common risk that is also, potentially, very costly if not covered. It's also not that expensive to insure against.

If you live in New Jersey, you might be able to offload some of these risks more cheaply by contracting your local mafia representative to take care of the offending party, but it's always wise to check first whether the mafia rate is a better value than the insurance rate. Sometimes the mafia is cheaper, but you have to be mindful of follow up "favors" they may request of you in the future.

As long as you keep your coverage focused on major, unaffordable, and realistic risks and you avoid coverage for smaller expenses you can afford to insure on your own, you're likely to get a good value from auto insurance.

Except in New Jersey.

Homeowner's insurance

Just as things can happen to your car, things can happen to your house. The roof might leak and cause a flood in the attic, destroying your priceless Van Gogh painting collection. Or maybe Great-Aunt Bergit will be visiting when she slips on a banana peel and sues you for the destruction of the priceless Van Gogh painting she carries around in her pocket. Maybe a hurricane strikes, and the wind knocks a tree into your living room, destroying the priceless Van Gogh painting you had hanging on the wall.

Literally anything could happen.

Unless you have the resources to cope with a major loss to your home and your art collection, you should have homeowner's insurance.

Homeowner's insurance has two main areas of protection. The first, obviously, is to your home and its contents. If your house is damaged or destroyed, the insurance carrier will step in and cover the damage. They also step in and cover the loss of the stuff inside the house, which can add up to a surprisingly large amount of money. As an added bonus, many homeowner's policies cover the value of your personal property anywhere in the world, so if you lose your Van Gogh painting while travelling, you might have coverage for it.

Of course, these policies often have limitations for rare or unusual personal property, so it's wise to check that first before assuming your paintings are covered.

The second area of protection is on liability. If someone trips on your sidewalk because you failed to repair the damage when little Billy spilled his Toddler's-First-Hydrofluoric-Acid-set all over it, or if little Billy left his train set lying near the door of your home right before your boss came to visit, causing him to trip and get disabled and wiping out his business, you could get sued for the injuries sustained. Even if you win the lawsuit, and there's no guarantee of that since little Billy is a terrible defense witness, the legal costs can be quite high. Having an insurance company provide a defense for you and pay for any damages awarded is a great way to get peace of mind.

Homeowner's insurance, while it costs more than the actual risk you're likely to face, isn't horribly inflated, and considering the financial consequence of a major lawsuit or a house fire, it's money well spent.

That doesn't mean it's infinitely valuable, though.

The most common claims are for small damages. If you agree to accept a high deductible and to pay for small damages yourself, the insurance carrier will generally give you a pretty nice price break. The larger the deductible and the more risk you take, the more you save.

If you're offered a range of deductibles from $500 to $10,000, you should elect the highest deductible you can afford to lose without hurting yourself financially. If a $1,000 loss is the most you could manage, start with that. As you build up your financial resources over time, you should also increase your deductible to reflect your extra capacity for self-insuring small losses until you get up to $10,000.

Most people, of course, don't have a choice about whether or not to have homeowner's insurance since it's a requirement if you also have a mortgage (and it's a reasonable value in any event), but you do have a choice about your deductible. A $10,000 loss would be no fun, but if you cut your premiums by $800 per year, you're likely to come out ahead over the long run.

Renter's insurance

If you don't own a home, renter's insurance provides similar benefits.

When a burglar breaks into your apartment and steals all of your Jim Nabors records, or when a friend "accidentally" drops a bottle of cesium in your garbage disposal and causes an explosion, you can suffer the loss of your property and potential lawsuits from your landlord.

Renter's insurance provides coverage on all of your worldwide belongings and liability protection in case someone sues you over something you failed to maintain in your home. While it provides no benefits for structures, that's okay because your evil, mustache-twirling landlord owns the structure, and he is able to obtain his own insurance policy on the structure itself when he's not busy ignoring the leaky water heater, raising your rent, and telling you you're not allowed to have a dog.

Not every landlord requires renter's insurance, but it's a really great idea to have it anyway. Premiums are really, really cheap (e.g., $20 per month for $100,000 in coverage), and while claims might be rare, it's an inexpensive way to get peace of mind over your stuff and any personal liability you might have for injuries caused at your home. Although renter's insurance, like all insurance, includes costs for insurance-company overhead, on such a cheap policy it doesn't really matter.

As with any insurance policy, you should elect the highest deductible you can afford to lose so as to minimize premiums. Deductibles are no fun, but at least you won't have any risk of catastrophic losses.

Title insurance

Title insurance is strange. Really strange. It's the kind of strange you might experience if the crack in the sidewalk by your house has an otherworldly, white glow coming out of it; strange, like a monkey riding a unicorn.

Unlike insurance you select to reduce your risks, title insurance is required whenever you get a mortgage, nobody really understands it, it provides risk reduction to a bank while you pay the premium, and the bank generally selects the policy and the provider.

In theory, title insurance is designed to provide protection in case you buy a house and it turns out the person who sold it to you didn't actually have proper title to it. For example, a man might own a house, and then he dies and leaves it to his three sons. One son lives in the house while the other two live elsewhere, and 40 years later, when the son in the house dies, his heirs sell the house to you.

If the paperwork wasn't done right when the father passed away decades ago, the other two sons, or their heirs if they passed away, might have a claim to the house you just bought. If they were to sue you and win the house back, you would lose the house and still be on the hook for the mortgage since the loss wasn't the bank's fault.

In another scenario, if you own some land and a neighbor claims part of it under adverse possession because he walked across it every day on the way to the bus stop for twenty years before you bought the property, you might lose that part of your land.

Other possible losses could include someone who forges the signature of the actual owner of a property and makes an unauthorized sale, or perhaps someone who subdivides a lot and messes up on the boundary paperwork.

These kinds of losses are extremely rare. By rare, I mean less than 1 in 1,000. But if you suffer the loss of your house because of a bad title, the consequences for you are bad, and the consequence for the bank that issued the mortgage to you is also bad. Having a title insurance company research the title before you make your purchase, or having them step in after the fact and take the loss when things go south, makes things much better for everyone, which is why banks require title insurance before issuing a mortgage.

Title insurance comes in two varieties: lender policies and owner policies.

The bank has you buy the lender policy to protect the bank. You can't do much about the required coverage, but if you're refinancing your mortgage and you paid for title insurance when you made the original purchase, the original title insurance company might give you a discounted "reissue" rate since they've already done the research work and they're not taking on any new risks. That begs the question of what, exactly, you're paying for on this reissued "insurance," but it's required, so it doesn't really matter that it provides no goods, services, or risk reduction.

For owner policies, you have the choice of taking the standard policy, taking an "enhanced" policy that covers you against extremely remote possibilities that probably never will happen, or taking no policy at all.

If the policy premiums were tied to actual risk, it might make sense to take enhanced coverage. Unfortunately, title insurance premiums are vastly inflated above the actual risk against which they protect you.

The process of buying a house involves mountains of indecipherable paperwork, made even more indecipherable as a bunch of people stare at you, tapping their fingers impatiently, waiting for you to sign everything, and making you feel guilty for wasting their time if you take the trouble to read what you're signing.

Nobody wants to read the details of a title insurance policy, so the bank usually picks the insurance carrier, and nobody cares. Many title insurance companies compete to get the bank's business, and while competition usually lowers prices, in this strange case competition actually causes prices to rise.

The lender is selecting the insurance carrier, but you're the one paying the premium. The lender doesn't care how much the insurance costs and you have to pay the cost, no matter what it is, so the title insurers have no incentive to compete by lowering premiums. Instead, they compete by raising premiums and giving rebates to the bank. Whoever has the highest premium can afford to give the largest rebate, and that's the company the bank chooses.

The title insurer works with agents to try and get the most bank business they can, and when the agent gets the bank to choose his company, he gets a percentage of the premium you pay. That percentage is often over 70%.

When 70% of your premium is going just to a commission before you even get to company overhead, you know the actual risk involved is miniscule and you're getting a lousy deal.

Although you're contractually stuck buying a lender's title policy, you do have the right to pick your own carrier (even if most people never bother). You can search online, and you might save a few hundred dollars for a few minutes of work.

The trickier question is whether or not to get the owner's policy. Although the risk is infinitesimal and the premiums expensive, it might be worth the expense when you make the purchase just so you have one less thing to worry about, especially since title insurance is a one-time expense instead of a monthly expense. On the other hand, if you want to save the money and take the risk yourself, you're probably going to be fine.

If you do decide to buy the owner policy, make sure you're getting the standard policy, and not the "enhanced" policy which the title company will probably try to sneak past you in the name of giving you "better" coverage you don't need. Also, if you refinance, don't buy a second owner's policy. It won't do anything that your original policy doesn't do, except cost you more money.

Life insurance

With most insurance, you want to be a winner. You want to get back some kind of benefit that's greater than the premiums you paid. It's not fun having a loss of some sort, but the insurance payout at least means you made a good decision in buying the insurance in the first place.

In the case of life insurance, you want to be a loser. You want to pay premium after premium, year after year, and you never want to get any kind of benefit in return. The only people who win with life insurance are people who die very quickly after buying. At least for me, there's nothing I want more than to lose 100% of my life-insurance investment.

Even though the objective with life insurance is to lose money, it still serves an extremely important purpose for many people.

If you have minimal assets but other people depend on your income, your untimely death could be devastating for your loved ones, or at least it could be devastating for the people who depend on your income (they're not always the same thing). You might have an ex-wife who depends on your income, for example, and if anything happens to you, you might be delighted at the thought of her falling into abject poverty and misery, which would serve her right after she decided to run off with the pool boy while abandoning you and winning an alimony judgment in the process.

But assuming you care about your family, you need to have a plan for how they'll get by if you die early. Do you expect your bereaved spouse to go to work? Do you have assets your family can depend on? Do you have 19 kids, but no reality TV show, and no idea how they'll eat, let alone go to college and pay off all the bad debts you left behind?

Life insurance fills the gap. In exchange for a premium each month, an insurance company will take care of your family if anything happens to you. Not having to worry about money for your family is quite a comfort.

Life insurance companies, unfortunately, make the process very complicated. They offer term life, whole life, universal life, variable life, and all sorts of variations and add-ons. The entire process is full of fees, commissions, and jargon designed to confuse you and your ability to assess what you actually need.

Here's the deal: Term life is the only thing you should ever consider. Term life is pure insurance. You pay a premium based on your age and health, and the insurance company gives your family a pile of money if you die. If you don't die, the policy ends, and that's all there is to it.

Every other variation takes that basic insurance product and confuses things by mixing it with a savings account or an investment account or tax considerations. Many years ago, before the advent of retirement plans, there were few ways to defer taxes on your investments. In that same era, estate taxes were quite high and with very low exemptions.

Life insurance has a special tax-code exemption that makes benefits tax free, and by mixing investments in with the insurance product, it becomes a way to avoid income taxes on your investments as well as avoiding estate taxes. That's pointless now for two reasons: 1) investment taxes can be easily deferred in retirement accounts, and 2) Federal estate taxes generally don't apply unless a couple has a net worth over $22 million. If your net worth is over $22 million, I really don't know why you're reading this book instead of consulting a skilled estate attorney.

The complicated life insurance products also work as a form

of "forced" savings, as much of the premium goes into building investment value, and in the old days before you could set up automatic bank transfers online, perhaps there was also some value in forcing yourself to build your net worth for your heirs. But now that it's so easy to automate money transfers, why bother with an inefficient and expensive way to make yourself save?

If you're interested in taking care of your family if something happens to you, get term insurance. If it's not term, don't bother looking at the details because it's a bad deal for everyone except the insurance company and the insurance salesman. As a fun fact, did you know that the salesman who sells a whole life policy often receives a commission equal to the first-year premium?

Term life insurance is quite simple. It's also quite inexpensive. Although the insurance company needs to cover its overhead costs like any other insurance company, competition in the term-life-insurance market has pushed premiums below the actual mortality risk they represent. That's possible for two reasons: 1) although everyone dies eventually, most people don't die before the policy expires, and 2) the insurance company earns investment income on your premiums before they have to pay out a death benefit.

As a result, you can get term insurance very cheaply. For example, a thirty-year-old man in good health can get a $500,000 policy that's good for twenty years for about $30 per month. Shorter terms are cheaper, longer terms are more expensive, lower benefits are cheaper, and higher benefits are more expensive.

Unlike other lines of insurance, the cost of life insurance increases as you get older. If you happen to develop any medical conditions as you age, which is a near certainty, your premiums increase even further. If you happen to get very sick, you become uninsurable, meaning that life insurance isn't available to you at any price. Once you've determined you need term life insurance, you should purchase a policy as quickly as possible.

The question then becomes how much coverage you need and for how long.

I suggest you should get a policy that remains in force until your youngest child is 21. After that, your children should be able to take care of themselves. If you've done your planning right, you should also have enough assets saved and invested to take care of your spouse by that point, although a spouse with no minor children also has great flexibility for working, if needed.

As for the coverage amount, I would suggest you set it high enough to cover all of your debts, including your mortgage, plus twenty times your non-housing expenses (your house would be paid off by the life insurance), minus whatever money and investments you already have.

For example, if you have a $300,000 mortgage, $50,000 in other debt, $30,000 per year in expenses besides your mortgage payment, and $100,000 saved in retirement accounts, then your coverage should be $300,000 + $50,000 + ($30,000 * 20) - $100,000 = $850,000. Obviously that's just a starting point. You can adjust it based on whether or not your spouse works, your lifestyle considerations, and whether you want your wife to become a merry widow living the high life when you're gone or whether you want her to toil in the salt mines weeping for her lost spouse.

For people who already have assets in excess of their insurance needs, life insurance is superfluous, and while it's safe to skip it, it won't really matter for you one way or another. For people who are single or who have no children, you might not need life insurance since there's nobody else depending on your income. For anyone else, term life insurance is a must have.

Garbage insurance (e.g., AFLAC and extended warranties)

I recently ordered a new toaster on Amazon, and they offered to sell me a two-year, extended warranty for 20% of the price of the toaster. Although I considered how sad my family would be if I were making toast, a fire ensued, and I died in the blaze without leaving behind toaster insurance, I declined the coverage.

The whole idea of insuring your toaster sounds ludicrous, and it is, but it's important to understand why it's ludicrous and why such a nonsensical product exists at all.

The whole point of insurance is to take small losses now, spread risk, and avoid potentially large, devastating losses in the future. It's a very useful and sensible system when reasonably priced for risk.

If your house burns down and you are stuck with a mortgage on a pile of smoking rubble, you could be financially ruined without an insurance company to take care of the loss. If you die in the fire and leave behind three orphans, your children could suffer mighty privation without a life insurance company to replace your lost income and provide the children with an enormous fortune that draws the envy of the notorious Count Olaf, who, by trying to steal the fortune, inflicts different privations upon your children.

If your orphaned children really enjoyed toast, but you didn't have an extended warranty on the toaster that melted in the fire, it's doubtful anyone could care about the lack of toaster insurance.

And yet people buy the toaster insurance.

It's really easy to get confused about when insurance is important and when it's not, people are really bad at estimating risk, and people are awful at estimating how difficult warranties are to use, so it should come as no surprise that many companies stand ready to offer products that don't make economic sense.

Obviously, somebody must be buying this stuff, or it wouldn't be peddled everywhere. And obviously it must be a big money-maker for the companies pushing it, because companies rarely push things that cause great losses for them. But there's no reason for you to be part of the fat profit margin on a wasteful product.

First, never ever get insurance on a loss you can afford to take. It would be a shame to have your new toaster go up in flames, but you can buy a new toaster. The same goes for losses on TVs, cell phones, blenders, and even the $1,000 deductible on your car insurance.

All insurance products have inefficient overhead built in to cover the administration and capital return of the insurance company. That doesn't mean that all insurance is bad or that it's not useful, but insurance is an inefficient product, so you should never buy more than you need. The more you can self-insure with your own emergency fund, the wealthier you'll be in the long run. As a practical matter, if the loss of some small object or trinket would cause you such financial hardship that you're seriously considering insurance for it, you probably shouldn't buy it, or at least you should buy a cheaper version.

Second, realize that the risks you're avoiding with insurance are less risky than you think. Although it's possible your kid might drop your phone in the blender, breaking both the phone and the blender and necessitating insurance claims on each, and although it's possible your new TV might suddenly stop working after a few months, these things are quite rare.

Obviously, nobody knows what the future holds, but there's a very easy way to measure the maximum risk you can expect: Take a look at the premium to insure against it.

If your cell phone cost $1,000 and the insurance costs you $150 per year, that means your chance of experiencing a loss on the cell phone is much less than 15% ($150 / $1,000, reduced by some amount for the overhead of the insurer). Or if your fancy coffee maker cost $100 and the insurance costs $20, the maximum chance of a loss is only 20%.

The actual chance of a loss is probably less than ½ of the amount you calculate based on the premium, because if it were any higher, the insurance company would go out of business. These are very small and remote risks.

Third, you don't know how hard it is to make a claim on the policy until you've already suffered a loss. While it's nice to know you have an extended warranty on your TV, once it actually breaks and you try to use the warranty, you'll find out that there's no coverage because you removed the plastic film that was on the screen when you first bought it, or perhaps you'll find out that you have to ship the TV to a repair center in China, where they'll charge you a $200 deductible and a return shipping fee, and if they approve your claim, which you won't know for sure until after you ship the TV, in 6-8 weeks you'll receive back a four-year-old, used TV because that's the depreciated value of the TV you insured.

Heaven help you if you ever try to make a claim on an extended warranty on a car. The list of exclusions on auto policies is so long as to make them nearly worthless. One of the worst cases I ever saw was someone who bought a brand-new car with a new-car warranty, and the car dealer successfully sold him an extended warranty on top of it. Not only was that extended warranty full of exclusions, but it was subordinate to the free warranty that was included with the new car, which meant that there was literally nothing the extended warranty would cover except for the vacations of the people running the company.

Insurance companies don't make money by sending out checks.

Don't think that garbage insurance is limited to extended warranties either. AFLAC famously advertises its duck who runs around yelling "AFLAC!" while people get money for rent or living expenses after getting sick or injured. That certainly sounds nice.

AFLAC is generally issued through the workplace, where you already have worker's compensation coverage or disability coverage in case you get sick or injured. And while AFLAC lists a long number of injuries or illnesses for which they make payouts, most of those are quite rare occurrences relative to the premiums they charge. What they're really trying to sell you is the idea of an emergency fund, but rather than recommending that you put away some money each month in case you have an emergency, money which you could keep if everything turns out okay, instead they recommend you put your money into a black hole with AFLAC, never to be seen again.

If you have a family history of cancer and you enjoy base jumping, maybe you'd come out ahead with AFLAC coverage, but everyone else is better off just sticking the AFLAC premiums into an emergency fund.

One of the funniest types of insurance is accidental death and dismemberment insurance. At a company where I worked, I was in charge of employee benefits, and this was one of the coverages provided. The idea of paying people $5,000 for losing one foot, $10,000 for losing two feet, or $10,000 for losing any two of a hand, foot, or eye, was quite silly. Not only is the loss of utility from losing two eyes far greater than twice the loss of utility from losing one eye, but the payouts were so small as to be meaningless. Further, dismemberment in an office setting is a rather rare occurrence for people who don't work for Dr. Frankenstein.

Although I wasn't the person who first added this "benefit" for the employees many years ago, I kept it in place for two reasons: 1) it was only $1 per month per employee, and 2) during lectures about employee benefits, I had fun discussing the payouts for losing hands, feet, and eyes, or the different ways you could become dismembered or killed in an office. A couple of bucks wasted on ludicrous insurance is worth it if you get some chuckles during a boring meeting at work.

So, if the insurance is fun, I guess that's a reason to get it, especially if you have an employer who's paying the bill, but otherwise you should avoid everything in this category.

Long-term care insurance

You know what's even less fun than being in a nursing home? Paying to be in a nursing home. Alzheimer's disease is the only saving grace. While that affliction doesn't make the nursing home any cheaper, it does reduce your awareness of the expense. On the plus side, most of the money to pay for the nursing home comes out of the inheritance for your kids, and let's face it: They never really visited often enough to deserve the money anyway.

I don't really fear the idea of a nursing home as much as people in the past might have. Certainly the expense is awful, as is declining health, but when you consider that much of your life is spent sitting on the couch in front of the TV, or sitting on a chair in front of the computer, or sitting in a car and operating a cell phone while you drive, as long as you still have the physical capacity to sit in front of something, the nursing-home life won't really be all that different from regular life. It'll just be more expensive.

The expense is a real issue, though, and to address it, some enterprising insurance companies came up with the idea of long-term care insurance.

Long-term care insurance is something you pay for when you're in your 50's to your 70's, and it kicks in when you're in your 80's or 90's and you need a nursing home. It'll often cover much of the cost, but the array of benefit levels, deductibles, options, and exclusions is mind boggling.

As is often the case with confusing insurance, all of those options are there to get you to buy more insurance. And as is the case with most insurance, you're more likely to lose than win (that's how the insurance company makes money), so you should buy only the minimum amount of insurance needed to offset risks you can't afford to take and skip all the other options.

It's helpful to step back and consider what you hope the long-term care insurance is going to do for you. If you're nursing-home bound and you run out of money, you're not going to be kicked into the street and forced to form an unlikely friendship with a band of plucky, street-smart youngsters who help you march along merrily on your trip to the grave. Instead, you'll stay in a nursing home while Medicaid kicks in and pays for your care. As a taxpayer, it would be nice to get an occasional card for providing that care to others, but somehow saying thanks always gets overlooked.

Thus, if you're very poor, you don't need long-term care insurance since the government will pay for your care.

If you're very rich, you also don't need long-term care insurance since you can pay for your care if you need it.

For people in the middle, there really isn't any risk of getting kicked out of the nursing home, so what you're insuring against is the risk of using up your money and having nothing to leave behind for your family. Long-term care insurance probably isn't the best way to do legacy planning, and there are a number of alternatives that make more sense.

Self-insure. During your working years, set aside money for your future. You should be doing that anyway. Part of your future may include a period of decrepitude, so set aside assets for that as well. If you need the money, it'll be there for you, and if you don't need the money because you live in perfect health, so much the better.

Consider your IRA. Long-term care premiums may be deductible, but when you consider the large standard deduction and the 7.5% of AGI hurdle before you can deduct medical expenses and long-term care premiums, it's highly unlikely you'll get much tax benefit from your insurance payments.

On the other hand, if you don't buy long-term care insurance and you use the savings to keep more money in your traditional IRA (e.g., taking smaller distributions or making larger contributions), you can simply take IRA distributions in years when you're in a nursing home.

Sure, the IRA distributions are taxable, but you'll have massive medical expenses available to itemize and offset your IRA distribution income. Effectively you'll be in a 0% tax bracket on IRA withdrawals. That's a great deal.

Consider term life insurance. Term life insurance is not counted against your Medicaid asset limit. If your goal is to leave something to your family, this is a much simpler process than the long-term care insurance. Just decide on how much money you want to guarantee for your family, pay annual premiums if you have the income, or perhaps a lump-sum premium if you're trying to use up assets, and consider that to be your kids' legacy while you spend down your other assets. Life insurance payouts are free of income and estate taxes, so that's another benefit as well.

If you want to go with life insurance, you should buy the policy at a younger age when you're in better health and premiums are more manageable, much the same way you would initially purchase a long-term care policy at a younger age. Life insurance is also available if you're old and sick, but the premiums involved at that point are quite high and you take on a much higher risk of a negative return if you live longer than expected.

Reverse mortgage. If you have a non-nursing-home-bound spouse, a reverse mortgage is a great option for freeing up capital to pay for your care without bumping against the complexity and inefficiency of insurance.

If none of these options is appealing to you, long-term care insurance is fine, but don't worry about getting a policy that covers 100% of all your future costs. You have no idea what things will cost in the future, and unused insurance is wasted. So don't even try to cover the full expense. Instead, buy a policy that covers some minimum amount. If you need more coverage down the road, you can pay for it out of other assets, comfortable in the knowledge that you at least reduced your expenses somewhat. If you don't need a nursing home at all, then at least you didn't waste too much money on premiums.

Some of the main reasons I'm not a big fan of these policies, besides the use-it-or-lose-it nature, is that they often have many exclusions and limitations built in, unpredictable premium increases, and benefits that don't necessarily provide as much coverage as you expect. Unpredictability is really bad in insurance.

Despite these challenges, I did consider long-term care insurance for myself. When I was 25, I figured that my extremely young age would get me a real bargain on coverage. Even if it weren't efficient, for $15 per month or some other trivial amount, at least it would be one less thing to think about for the future.

The insurance companies, in the face of my application, came through with all the disappointment I could have hoped for: They quoted me a premium for a 50-year-old because they had no idea how to price policies for my age. Suffice it to say, I did not sign up. My wife, however, enjoyed making fun of me for planning a nursing home stay 50 or 60 years before I might actually need one.

As long as you have a backup plan for nursing-home finance (which could include leaving nothing for the kids or going on Medicaid), you're probably better off keeping your finances simple and self-insuring.

Health insurance

This is the big one.

A huge percentage of people's income gets devoured here, whether you pay premiums directly for an individual plan or whether you get the plan through work (which is part of your income even if you never see the money). Health insurance is an emotional topic, and one that comes up regularly in political discourse.

Emotion and politics are really bad when you're making long term financial plans, so you have to force yourself to step back and evaluate health insurance rationally while you work through your decision making. Simply saying that you need it or that it's expensive and that the government should pay isn't an analysis.

It's important to remember that health insurance doesn't actually have anything to do with your medical care or your health. The insurance doesn't treat you or make you healthy when you're sick. The doctors and pharmaceuticals and labs and hospitals are the ones who do that. The insurance is really just a tool to help you pay for the medical bills so that you can keep your money available for other priorities, because, really, I think most people would rather spend money on anything besides a colonoscopy.

Health insurance is a weird financial product, though. Whereas the vast majority of people are never going to experience a house fire, almost 100% of people are going to experience medical expenses at some point in their lives. The exact magnitude and timing of the medical expenses is unknown, but declining health is a certainty in life. Annual checkups and lab work, routine care, and other regular expenses are also to be expected.

In that sense, health insurance is really more of a prepaid expense on a long-term installment plan rather than real insurance offloading a risk onto someone else. You're just paying in advance for something you'll have to pay for anyway down the road.

But it gets weirder. Since the majority of health insurance comes through employers who don't tell their employees the full cost of the insurance, and since it also comes tax free, employees have the incentive to consume as much health care as they possibly can and to push as many prepaid expenses into the plan as possible.

In no way does it make sense to get insurance for a $150 dental cleaning that you know you'll be doing every six months, but if your employer is paying the premiums and the government is making it tax free, then suddenly it's a great thing to push that into an insurance product rather than getting the money directly and paying taxes before paying the dentist.

This has the effect of artificially increasing the demand for an insurance product that isn't really insurance, and thus increasing the cost. It also has the effect of people confusing medical care with medical insurance and how you should pay for something you know you'll need anyway. If someone suggests you have to pay $600 for new tires, you don't complain because you know you need the tires, but if you're told you have to pay $150 at the dentist for a cleaning, it's as if that person said he likes throwing puppies off skyscrapers for fun. "I should pay for a dental cleaning?! No! The insurance should pay for it!"

The reality is that insurance is already a bloated tool for actual risk reduction even under the best of circumstances, and when you interlard it with prepaid expenses, you get a really inefficient mess.

It gets weirder still.

Ideally, insurance works because the insurer collects small payments from a large number of people, and they use that to pay for the really big losses incurred by a small number of people, plus company overhead. But because health insurance has so many prepaid expenses crammed into it, the insurance company has to take a large amount of money from a large number of people in order to pay for small expenses for lots of people in addition to large expenses for a few people.

Then the government comes along and says, "your health insurance is too expensive; we'll create a new system for insurance risk pooling and set more rules and requirements on the insurance companies," which has the effect of increasing insurance overhead, adding more government overhead, and shifting costs around from one employer pool to the next.

When costs rise further in response to this additional overhead, the insurance companies put mandates on doctors and hospitals to cut costs and bill in more detail, which increases the overhead costs for the providers, which then pushes prices and premiums up more.

Then the government comes along again and says, "health insurance is more expensive. Obamacare will make it cheaper!" The government then mandates that insurance companies can't price premiums based on risk, which makes premiums rise, but the government offsets this by giving subsidies to reduce some people's premiums while taking more money from other people based on income, which of course requires more overhead to manage.

Thus, the insurance gets heaping layers of overhead added on to a system for redistributing wealth that's based on income instead of risk so that it can reshuffle who pays for expenses that people know they'll have to pay anyway.

This is not insurance. It's a farce.

If you get insurance through an employer, chances are you don't have a choice about it. A large portion of your compensation will go to health insurance whether you like it or not, and there isn't a decision for you to make.

If you buy insurance on your own, you do have a choice, especially since there's no longer any individual mandate.

In both cases, the starting point you want, as with any real insurance, is to have the highest deductible you can afford to lose in a given year. That minimizes your premiums and your expected overhead losses. If the insurance plan is health savings account compatible, that's even better since the health savings account is a wonderful, tax-advantaged tool.

Yes, the high-deductible plans are going to force you to pay for more small expenses on your own, but it is highly inefficient to pay premiums to cover small expenses that you think you're likely to pay anyway rather than just paying for the small expenses yourself. Worse yet is paying premiums to cover small expenses, like routine dental visits, and then not even going to the dentist.

Pay for as much of your own medical care as you can. I promise you the dentist won't look down upon you as some kind of inferior subspecies simply because you pay your own bills. And your bank account will thank you in the long run for choosing the more efficient option, even if it is the scarier option.

The exception to this, of course, is if you have chronic medical conditions or other major expenses on the horizon. That falls into the category of being riskier than the insurance company expects, in which case you want to get the most insurance you possibly can since you're laying off known losses on someone else. Very sick people or people who anticipate major medical expenses like surgery or childbirth should also get the lowest possible deductibles.

For healthier people, sometimes even having no health insurance makes sense. While health care is important and health insurance, by extension, is also important, the value of the insurance is not infinite. If you have the option for your family medical expenses to be fully covered with no deductibles for $50 per month, that'd be a great deal. Even at $100 or maybe even $1,000 per month, it could make sense. If you have a $10,000 deductible and a premium of $2,000 per month, does that make sense? Maybe, but probably not. What if the premium were $10,000 per month or $1 million per month? At a certain point it is obviously cheaper to pay for your own medical costs than to buy insurance.

So, if health insurance isn't worth an infinite premium, then there's some ceiling for its value. That ceiling is different for everyone, but there's always a point at which being uninsured and paying for expenses yourself is the right decision. The fact that the insurance has the word "health" in it does not confer any magical properties upon it that make it somehow more essential than air or more valuable than the riches of Croesus. It's still a financial decision like any other.

One of the bizarre features of Obamacare is that all insurance is guaranteed issue, and it can't take into account preexisting conditions, such as heart disease or pregnancy. If you don't currently have insurance, you can always wait until you get sick before you sign up, and thus save the premiums. It's sort of like waiting until your house is on fire before you buy homeowner's insurance, and then getting a new house thanks to government mandates!

While it's true that Obamacare has only limited enrollment periods each year, there's always an enrollment period on the horizon. The worst-case scenario is that you need to be prepared to pay for 11 months of medical costs before the insurance kicks in. That's potentially expensive, but likely far less expensive than the premiums you save year after year.

There are even ways to take this further. If you are uninsured and you find yourself suddenly in need of an enormously expensive operation which can't be put off until the next open-enrollment period, you can always get married or divorced, which triggers a new enrollment period for you. Then you buy your insurance, get your procedure, have the insurance company pay for it, and get divorced or remarried, depending on what you did to trigger the enrollment period.

This whole concept, of course, is stupid. But it's the law of the land, and until the law changes, there's nothing inherently immoral with using the tools our omniscient legislators brought forth with great thought and care.

So the only question then, is whether or not it makes sense to buy health insurance if you don't have it. Since health insurance premiums are tied to income and not risk, then health insurance becomes a better value as your income goes down and your subsidies go up, and it becomes a worse value as your income rises and the insurance acts like an additional tax.

If your income is low and you don't have the resources to pay for 11 months of medical expenses in a worst-case scenario, then it probably makes sense to buy health insurance since the government is offloading the risk for you. If your income is very high and you are able to cover 11 months of medical expenses, then you're effectively paying an abnormally high premium to subsidize other people, and it doesn't make sense to buy health insurance.

Similarly, if you're much sicker than an average person, then preexisting-condition protections mean other people are paying for your risk, and it makes sense to buy health insurance. If you're very healthy, it doesn't make sense to buy since you're not getting any cost reduction from your good health and low risk.

Unfortunately, there's no clear place to draw the line between worth it and not, so you have to make a judgment call based on your own financial resource level, health expectations, expected income, government subsidies, and risk tolerance. The good thing at least is that if you make the wrong decision, you can always change your mind later without penalty.

CHAPTER 14:
CREDIT CARDS: GOOD OR EVIL?

Superman movies are always a lot of fun. I can't remember if it was Superman II or Superman III, but there was a part where Superman was about to stop Lex Luther before the culmination of his evil plan, when suddenly Luther found a way to stop Superman: issue him a credit card.

Superman got distracted by the high credit limit and the ease with which he could buy stuff, and he racked up thousands of dollars of high-interest debt while buying designer capes. Instead of fighting the bad guy, a job which doesn't pay enough to cover those finance charges, Superman was forced to work long hours at the Daily Planet writing articles about third-grade bake sale fundraisers.

With Superman hobbled by credit-card debt, Luther conquered the world and enslaved humanity.

Spoiler alert: If you didn't watch Superman II or Superman III, credit cards didn't actually enter into the movie at all. That's because credit cards aren't inherently evil. They are tools that can be used for good purposes or for bad purposes, just like a hammer, a baseball bat, or an alligator. It all depends on what you choose to do with them.

Credit cards also weren't in the movie because they would have made the movie extremely boring as audiences watched Superman try to figure out his budget, pay bills, and spend hours on hold with customer service while Metropolis burned to the ground.

When used judiciously and with full awareness of your budget, credit cards have many wonderful and redeeming features. New accounts often come with large sign-up bonuses. Many accounts earn cash back or travel points. Every credit card also gives you more use of your own money for free, both from the time you make the charge until the statement closes, and also from the time the statement closes until the interest-free grace period ends.

Sometimes you can have almost two months with no interest before you need to pay for your purchase. Often that can be combined with 0% promotions from the bank that extend for several additional months. While it's not a good habit to depend on paying for things later, it never hurts to have the option.

There are many other benefits. In the case of fraud, you can dispute the transaction with your bank, and it's very easy to get your money back without having to wait. Even if there's no fraud, you can often dispute a charge from a business that isn't delivering the goods or services you paid for, and the bank will be on your side to help you keep your money.

For recordkeeping, it's great to have an itemized list of your spending. And there can also be ancillary benefits depending on the specific card, such as extended warranty protections, extended return periods, auto-rental insurance, and so forth.

The downsides of credit cards are, of course, more obvious. Interest rates are usually usurious if you carry a balance and know what usury is. If you don't know what usury is, then you just get charged very high interest rates, sometimes approaching 30%. While that number looks big, consider what it means in practical terms: Everything you buy doubles in cost within 2.5 years.

Interest at that rate can severely damage your ability to save for your future. If you can't get the balance paid down, your debts grow over time and you get trapped in debt, potentially leading to bankruptcy. And while you might intend for this not to happen, credit cards make spending extremely easy for people who are not naturally inclined to save or watch their budgets.

The question you have to ask yourself before using credit cards is what kind of person you are. Are you the kind of person who is highly organized, cautious in your spending habits, and exceedingly self-controlled? Then credit cards are a wonderful tool that adds benefits and flexibility to your financial life. On the other hand, if you're naturally impulsive, disorganized, and inclined to spend money like Congress on the slightest whim, then you probably should avoid credit cards.

There's no shame in using debit cards or cash for your transactions. Knowing yourself and your own limitations is one of the most empowering things you can add to your life.

Getting started with credit

Everyone should own a credit card. Not everyone should use a credit card. You could be the most impulsive and careless person in the world, and simply having a credit card isn't going to make you more inclined to spend. The credit card isn't going to run out the door by itself and start making purchases, nor is the credit card going to sneak onto your computer at night, guess your password, and start ordering tons of anime figurines.

For people who lack self-control, it might be advisable to lock away the credit card somewhere hard to reach, like a bank safe-deposit box or the jaws of your pet shark. You might consider cutting it to pieces while leaving the account open. Maybe you have a favorite finance author you like enough to hold the credit card for you, and who promises not to use it for anything unless it's really important, and who absolutely will pay you back eventually.

The point isn't so much having a credit card to use as it is to have the account open in the first place, and this is something you want to do as soon as possible.

At some point in most people's lives, they need to borrow money for something. Most commonly it's to buy a car or a house. Some people borrow money to buy thousands of copies of their favorite personal finance book. But in all cases, you need to have a good credit score to get the best rates.

One of the elements of a credit score is your average age of accounts. Put another way, banks want to see that you've been able to keep a debt account open for a long time, and the longer the better. Even if you never use your credit card, having it open for a long time makes it easier and cheaper to borrow money in the future when the need arises. Picking out a card with no annual fee means there's really no downside to seasoning your credit report with a credit card.

Contrary to popular belief, there's no need to carry a balance in order to improve your credit score. You might consider making a purchase once a year or every other year to keep your account active (even a piece of gum is enough) since some banks will close credit cards that haven't been used in a long time, but that's about the only usage requirement.

If you choose to use credit

If you decide you're comfortable with paying for most purchases on credit, that's great! There are a number of tips to consider:

1. Never charge anything you can't afford to pay off at the end of the month. If you can't pay the bill in full, then you should stop buying stuff. Even a single month of high interest wipes out all the rewards and benefits that come from credit usage.

2. Open a rewards card. There are numerous varieties of rewards cards available, some of which generate airline miles or hotel points, others which give store credits, and some which give cash back. Unless you really understand the relative value of the points you're generating, stick with cash back as the simplest option. The Citibank DoubleCash card is a convenient option that pays 2% back with no annual fee, for example. What's not to like about getting a 2% discount on every single thing you buy?

3. Never buy something you don't need to get a credit-card reward. The needless spending wipes out the benefit of the reward.

4. The interest rate on the credit card doesn't matter if you never carry a balance. Don't bother opening a credit card because of the interest rate. Open a new credit card only if the reward structure on the new card is better than the one on your current card, or if it complements the structure of your current card in some way. If it takes you more than a minute to understand how your credit reward structures fit together, then stick with a single card for simplicity.

5. Don't be afraid to call your credit-card issuer and ask for things. If you missed a payment, ask for them to waive the late fee. If your interest rate is very high, ask for a lower rate. If you have an annual fee, ask for a waiver or promotion or retention offer. The worst thing that can

happen is they'll say no, but often they'll give you something if you ask nicely. There's no reason not to do this as long as you have something specific you want to request. The only exception would be if you're calling to ask for a date, because, let's face it, a credit-card company probably makes for a lousy date.

6. If you have a prior credit-card debt you can't pay off right away, it's okay to open a new credit card with a 0% rate and then to transfer the balance. The balance transfer may have an upfront fee of 2% or 3%, but if it saves you 18% for a year, you come out way ahead. The key for making this work is twofold: 1) set a reminder for when the promotional rate comes due, and 2) have a plan for how to pay off the debt before the promotional rate expires. If you make a balance transfer and fall into the habit of not paying, or if you fall back into a 20% interest rate, you erase all of your progress.

Credit card usage can be a very useful tool when used wisely, but if you don't fully understand what you're doing or if you're unsure of your own level of self-control, just avoid credit cards altogether. It's better to give up the benefits of a credit card than it is to fall into a trap of high-interest debt.

CHAPTER 15:
RETIREMENT

One of my coworkers many years ago continued coming into the office every day even though he was 79 and had a government pension. He enjoyed the work, but every single time we went to lunch, after he finished telling me about his work in the Ford administration, he also said that all of his friends who retired and moved to Florida died within two years, and he wasn't keen on the idea.

Then there's a friend of mine took an opposite approach to retirement. He spent time as a student or otherwise doing nothing from the ages of 20 to 40. He considered that as his retirement, and he had a grand old time. Then he spent the next part of his life trying to catch up, until job circumstances later on forced him to retire again at 63. Luckily for him, he was bailed out just in time with an inheritance.

Most people, though, prefer to avoid the extremes and retire in the range of 55 to 65. Maybe that comes from good planning, but mostly it's just a function of working until you can't work anymore and making do with whatever you happened to set aside.

Retirement really should be a choice. There's enough effort and emotional strain involved in the transition from full-time work to full-time freedom, and making that transition at a random time with random resources only compounds the strain. If the goal is to reduce your stress in life, it begins with early planning to build up your resources and introspection about your goals.

Generally, you should target a retirement age that's lower than you think is reasonable. That's important for several reasons.

First, retirement due to job loss or health is extremely common (perhaps even the most common reason people retire), and if you're prepared at a younger age to walk away from work, then health issues and job losses are less of a big deal when they force themselves upon you.

Second, aiming to call it quits at a younger age forces you to plan ahead sooner and save more, both of which give you more options down the road if something goes wrong. If your plan is to work until you die while spending everything along the way, even the smallest obstacle is a disaster.

Third, and probably most significant, the shorter time horizon for planning increases the urgency of planning and saving under Parkinson's Law. Parkinson's Law is the old adage that the amount of time required to do a job increases to fill the time allotted.

If you needed a week to write a paper in school and you were given two weeks, chances are you did nothing for the first week and then finished it up in the second week. If you were given two months to finish the paper, probably you would have done nothing for the first seven weeks and then spent the last week cramming in all work finishing the paper.

Even for projects at work, the same thing happens: People make an estimate of the actual time they need for completing a job, and then they begin the project at the last possible minute. It might make more sense to start when the project is assigned, but nobody does that.

It sounds like a joke, but this is just human nature. It's how people prioritize. And the same thing applies to retirement.

Let's say it takes 25 years of serious saving and investing to reach your retirement goal. If you're 20 years old and you plan to retire at

80, you have 60 years to prepare, which means you'll mess around and spend all your money for the first 35 years before panicking and struggling for the next 25 years to get your finances in order. However, if you plan to retire at 45, you'll struggle and save as much as you can for 25 years, at which point your choices will be 1) continue working for fun, 2) become richer, 3) increase your spending without guilt, or 4) actually retire at 45.

Setting your retirement goal when you're young is wonderful, but if you're no longer young (which applies to everyone except my wife, who turns 29 every year) and if you're behind where you want to be financially, you still have several levers you can pull: spend less, earn more, reduce your retirement budget, change investments, and work longer.

Spending less and earning more both increase your savings rate, which helps you to catch up on your goals more quickly. How you do that is a personal decision, but it moves you in the right direction, at least.

Reducing your retirement budget has the effect of lowering your goal, which makes the goal easier to achieve at the expense of your retirement lifestyle. Most people don't care for that tradeoff, but sometimes it's the only way to get by and you do what you have to do.

Changing your investments to take on more risk (principally by buying more stocks) can help you reach your goal faster with higher investment returns, and more often than not it'll help, but there's no guarantee. There's also a limit on how much risk is reasonable to take on in a desperate attempt to reach your retirement goal. Increasing your stock allocation from 60% to 70% is fine. Betting on the pass line at the craps table is not.

The final option, working longer, is the most powerful tool in your arsenal. Each additional year of working has three benefits: you save more money, your investments have more time to grow, and you shorten the number of retirement years you need to fund.

Generally, you'll want to use some combination of all these tools to get you to where you need to be. The exact mix is a personal decision, but the good news is that there are always options.

For people naturally inclined to save, there are additional challenges for retirement. If you're used to saving money, quitting your job and going into a retirement drawdown mode is a major change. Stepping aside after years of building your net worth is difficult when another year of working helps you save, grow your investments, increase your pension or Social Security benefit, and lower your long-term expenses.

Working and saving and investing for an extra year might help you grow your retirement income by an additional $5,000 per year. And working another year after that might add another $5,000. And working a year after that might add another $5,000. Although each year of extra work makes you financially better off, you could play that game forever and reach the end of your life with a gigantic retirement income you never used.

At a certain point, once you've reached your goals plus a margin of error, you just have to say, "that's enough," and walk away from adding to the pile. Sure, you could grow your net worth more if you work more, but if the extra money won't do anything to improve your lifestyle, then money should no longer be a priority. You could continue working if you enjoy it or if your spouse wants you out of the house so she can spend time with her "friend," who, coincidentally, happens to look a lot like your kids, but you shouldn't let money be a factor in the decision.

For most people, the question of what to do when you have more money than you need isn't likely to come up, but if it does, it's a happy problem to have.

The question you're more likely to face is your vision for your own life. Without the predictability of a regular work schedule to fill up your day, retirement presents a blank slate with vast quantities of time to fill up. Other than summer breaks in childhood, most people aren't prepared for how to approach this new-found freedom. Unfortunately, your past experience from summer breaks isn't going to be terribly helpful unless you enjoy video games and skateboarding.

It's often good to find something fun and productive to do with your time. This is a highly personal area. Some people continue working, some people volunteer, and others travel or spend more time with family, but whatever you choose, the great thing about achieving your financial goals is that you don't have to rush to find an answer, you don't have to be motivated by money, and you'll potentially find more enjoyment in life. The only person who will find less enjoyment is your wife while you sit around every day asking her what's for lunch.

Social Security

Social security taxes suck up 12.4% of your income while you're working. It might appear to be only 6.2% when you look at your paycheck withholding, but your employer pays a matching 6.2% tax on your salary, money that makes you more expensive to employ and which could otherwise be paid to you as additional salary.

If you earn $50,000 per year, you're paying $6,200 annually in Social Security taxes. If you invested that money at 7%, after a 40-year career, you'd have amassed $1.24 million, which would comfortably produce $50,000 per year in income forever while leaving the original principal for you to leave to your heirs. Since you don't actually get to invest your tax money, instead the $1.24 million goes into a government black hole never to be seen again, while your $50,000 in annual investment income instead comes back to you as a $21,000 Social Security benefit.

That is a pretty lousy deal. Unfortunately, it's the deal we have to live with.

It could very easily get worse. Social Security is famously on very poor financial footing. Most likely taxes are going to go up while benefits go down. It wouldn't be surprising if benefits disappear entirely for people with income above a certain level, or for people who worked hard to save and invest for their futures and have some money saved up.

Unless you're within 15 years of retirement age, it's best to plan for your Social Security benefit to be nothing and to save and invest accordingly. Maybe you'll be surprised and get a benefit that's greater than nothing. If that's the case, nobody ever got hurt having more money than expected. But the critical thing is to make sure that your retirement plans are not dependent on government largesse. You need to be able to provide for yourself regardless of what Congress does, and, let's face it, Congress is notorious for disappointing people.

If you're close to retirement age, you're probably going to receive a Social Security benefit that's close to what you expect, and it's okay to take that into account in your plans based on the high likelihood of receiving it. In that case, you have a few decisions to make about how you want to receive it.

The primary decision involves when to take the benefit. You can claim Social Security benefits as early as age 62, or as late as age 70. If you claim benefits early, you get your income earlier, but it's reduced significantly and you get penalized with further benefit reductions if you continue working. If you take benefits at age 70, you get significantly higher benefits, but you'll be older and you won't live to receive it for as many years.

The decision about the best age for claiming is fairly complex, doubly so if you're married and you have a spouse who can claim a benefit based on your earnings record, or if you and your spouse have significantly different ages. The rules also change from time to time, and while you should consider seeking advice on this topic, there are a few basic guidelines you can follow.

You should consider claiming benefits early if:
1. You're in very poor health,
2. You plan to save the money from your benefit and invest it, and
3. You're not actively working.

You should consider claiming benefits late if:
1. You're in excellent health,
2. You're actively working, and
3. Your savings and investments aren't where you need them to be, and the higher benefit would help you to meet your future income needs.

You might also consider claiming benefits early for lifestyle reasons. For example, perhaps you're working at a job you hate and with people you hate, while every day suffering a commute you hate. You want nothing more than to escape your world of misery. If your existing investments don't quite generate enough income to cover your lifestyle, but claiming Social Security benefits early would give you that extra income you need to be able to call it quits, there's absolutely nothing wrong with forgoing extra money in the future in order to make your life better starting at an earlier age.

As with most personal finance decisions, there is no right or wrong answer about when to claim Social Security benefits. This is a personal decision and value judgement as much as a financial one.

Asset drawdown rates

Once upon a time, a little girl named Goldilocks wandered through the forest and found a small cabin. She walked inside and found three financial plans on the table. She looked at the financial plan for Papa Bear, who planned to consume 15% of his assets each year. "This one's too aggressive," said Goldilocks. "He'll run out of money within seven or eight years." She read the financial plan for Mama Bear, who planned to consume 1% per year. "This one's too conservative," she said. "Mama Bear is going to forego her retirement lifestyle in exchange for preserving assets she doesn't need."

Then she looked at the financial plan for Baby Bear. "This one is just a mess of crayons and scribbles. It looks like Baby Bear doesn't even have a plan, like me! This one is just right."

Goldilocks looked again at the plans and copied off the Social Security numbers and dates of birth. She walked through the cabin, collecting all the jewelry and valuables, and escaped into the forest, where she came across a magic fox who ran a no-questions-asked pawn shop. She then opened up some credit card accounts in the Bears' names and escaped with a big pile of money.

When Goldilocks retired, she spent her money too quickly and became destitute because her asset drawdown plan was a mess of scribbles and crayons.

When you're working and saving money, the goal is to set a high-enough savings rate and grow your money. Once you quit working, the calculus flips entirely and you have to figure out a safe rate at which to draw down your assets while keeping reasonably sure they'll never run out. Unlike Goldilocks, you want to have a plan to make sure you don't consume your money too fast or too conservatively.

This is tricky as well since you can reasonably expect your expenses to increase over time with inflation.

There were three professors at Trinity University (no, they weren't bears) who produced a study in 1998 that looked at investment returns from 1925 through 1995. They looked at various allocations of stocks and bonds to see what the chances were that such a portfolio would hold up over a 30-year period without being exhausted.

The conclusion was that for a stock-heavy portfolio, you could safely withdraw 4% of your portfolio's initial value and increase that every year for inflation with a very low likelihood of your money running out. There's a great deal of debate over whether the 4% rule is excessively conservative or excessively stupid, and many personal finance experts feel very strongly one way or another. My view is that the 4% rule is an excellent and simple starting point which doesn't need to be followed as an absolute.

If you begin your retirement by consuming 4% of your retirement assets, there's no law that says you have to continue increasing that amount every year for 30 years. If you have a really bad year for your investments, most people would likely respond by lowering their spending for that year. If you have several bad years in a row, perhaps you'd find ways to lower your spending permanently. The idea of robotically spending more regardless of how you're doing is contrary to human nature, and the idea that you'd keep increasing your spending each year even as your assets march down to zero is ludicrous.

The rule also can be adjusted somewhat based on age. For example, if you retire at 50 instead of 65 and have to fund an extra 15 years of retirement, you might consider consuming 3.5% of your initial retirement assets each year. Conversely, if you retire at 75, you might choose to consume 6%. You could also consider increasing or decreasing your starting rate by an additional 0.5% or 1% based on whether you wish to be more conservative or more aggressive with your investments, but that really is about the limit on the range of reasonable withdrawal rates. Anything significantly higher comes with the risk that you'll run out of money in the future, and anything lower means you're not spending as much as you could (although if you're happy spending less, that's okay).

If you have ample retirement assets, you might also consider lowering the aggressiveness of your investments or holding more cash, while also lowering your withdrawal rate. For example, maybe your lifestyle costs you $60,000 per year, and your investments generate $75,000 per year in investment income.

If your aggressive investments pay off, maybe your income would jump to $90,000 per year. But unless you want to lease a new Lamborghini or fly first class, the extra money won't do anything for you when you're already happy with how you live. However, if your aggressive investments fail, you might be left with only $50,000 per year in income, at which point you couldn't fund your lifestyle fully and you would be worse off.

Why risk what you have and need for something you don't need?

A fully-funded retirement that more than covers your lifestyle gives you the flexibility to invest less aggressively if you so choose. That might mean holding less speculative stocks or more cash, and while you would undoubtably grow your money more slowly in the process, you also would have a lot less to worry about, which itself is pretty valuable.

Unfortunately, there's no absolute number that dictates the correct amount to withdraw based on age or the correct amount of risk to take. There's a necessary element of guesswork involved; guesswork can't be escaped any more than death or a nagging wife.

There are some ways to boost the odds in your favor, though. The Trinity Study looked at portfolios that included some portion in bonds. That made sense at the time since bonds paid something. Bonds presently pay nothing, so currently they should be avoided entirely. Since that leaves you with an all-stock portfolio, you're likely to generate higher returns over the long run.

Although an all-stock portfolio is more volatile, that can be mitigated somewhat if you have a cash fund that covers 6-12 months of living expenses. In the event of a stock crash, having the option to draw down cash instead of selling stocks at a low point is a wonderful way to bring peace of mind and wait out the bad times.

You can also mitigate risk further if you're willing to accept some volatility in your income. Focusing on stocks that pay safe, sustainable dividends lets you base your annual spending on whatever your dividend income happens to be. Most companies increase their dividends over time, which provides you with inflation protection, and a reliance on dividend cash flow means you don't have to rely on unpredictable capital gains. Even in a bad year when markets drop and dividends fall, you can avoid selling any of your stocks during the market bottom if you cut your spending to match the reduction in your dividend income. That gives you a chance to wait out the eventual recovery without panic.

Of course, a dividend-focused strategy doesn't have to be all or nothing. It's great if your dividends cover all your expenses, but even if they cover only most of your expenses, the need to panic during crashes is limited.

For example, if you target a 4% withdrawal rate, but your investments pay 2.5% in dividends, then you're on the hook to sell only 1.5% of your portfolio principle each year. During market crashes those sales would still be at a low prices, but the effect of making only small sales during market crashes is as insignificant as a professional football player conducting quantum physics research, which is to say, not very significant.

F.I.R.E – Good or evil?

F.I.R.E stands for Financial Independence Retire Early. It's a movement chock full of people who shun the standard American lifestyle of working, paying taxes, spending all your money on stuff you don't need, and repeating until you die. Instead, adherents aim to save as much of their income as they can, sometimes 50% or more each year, invest, and get out of the workforce in their 40's or 50's with a modest, but financially-independent lifestyle.

This movement is based on the fundamental question of what wealth means to you. Does wealth mean your capacity to maximize the buying of expensive stuff, or does wealth mean your capacity to maximize the independent use of your time? Would you rather work longer and have more money and less time, or would you rather retire early and have more time and less money?

There's no right or wrong answer.

For people who would rather have more time than money, the key to success is to live way below your means so as to maximize your savings. When your friends and coworkers are living the high life, they might look at you like you're crazy if you choose to drive an old car instead of a new, shiny one, or if you decide to live in a small apartment instead of a large house, or if you choose to cook your own food instead of dining out, or if you end up taking a camping vacation instead of a tour of Europe. But people who set a goal of financial independence usually don't care what other people think. Not coincidentally, a very large amount of personal spending is based on impressing other people, and if you're the type of person who doesn't care to impress other people, saving money often comes quite easily.

There's really nothing else to it. If you live modestly and consistently manage a 50% savings rate, retiring by age 45 or 50 is very easy with just average investment returns.

Even if your savings rate isn't so high that you can afford to "Retire Early" and leave the workforce in your 40's, a superior savings rate still enables you to enjoy "Financial Independence."

A large investment portfolio kicking off consistent dividend income gives you more choices even before you reach your final goals. You might currently hate your life, suffering daily in a soul-stealing job with miserable coworkers and an awful commute, but if you have the option to tell your boss to go pound sand while you escape to another job that you might find more enjoyable or personally fulfilling, even if it pays less, it really takes off the pressure. Or if you like your job and your boss isn't the Antichrist, financial independence could help you to work fewer hours and spend more time with your kids. Maybe you wouldn't change anything, and instead you'd simply enjoy less stress in your life since you don't have to fret about money.

If you find that you're happier working more hours for more years so you can spend more money, there's nothing automatically wrong with that option either. It's a personal choice, and the whole point of financial independence is to have choices. There's nothing worse being trapped in a job and a commute and hours you hate so you can toil for years paying down debt and living beyond your means to impress people you don't care about.

F.I.R.E. gets a bad rap in some circles, though, because of articles that pop up and misuse the term. I've seen some stories with titles like, "How I Retired at 32," or "Man Retires at 29 and Travels the World," and they always start by talking about F.I.R.E. and what it means.

As you get into the story, you find out that the guy who retired at 32 did it by selling his software company to Google for $8.2 million, and now that he "retired," he has time to run his new consulting business, give paid lectures, and market copies of his new book series while his wife enjoys her time running a successful neurology practice. Meanwhile, the guy who "retired" at 29 to travel the world actually saved only $85,000, is single with no kids, and limits his international travel to Canada.

Although the internet is usually very accurate, stories like these are highly misleading because you're not really "retired" when you're still running a business and your wife is working, or when your nest egg is just barely enough to take a little time off from work. These articles also talk about funding your 401(k) or cutting your morning coffee as the ways to achieve early-retirement goals, but when you highlight someone who did something extremely uncommon like founding a software company in his 20's that he sold for millions of dollars, none of this is really "retirement" in a way that makes sense to anyone, and it gives the whole lifestyle a bad name.

There are also other people who have more substantive complaints: The only way to retire early is by living a miserable lifestyle and never having kids; early retirement isn't realistic for most people; retiring early and with a low income gets you huge health insurance subsidies, which isn't fair to everyone else; with a long retirement, you don't have any margin of error in case something goes wrong.

While there are elements of truth to all these points, the same concerns are relevant whether you're aiming to retire at 40 or 70. Retiring early isn't the question. The real question is what tradeoffs you're willing to make in your life, and what your lifestyle preferences are. Those are personal choices, and there's nothing morally wrong with giving up some things and quitting at an earlier age instead of a later one.

The only complaint that I find completely invalid is the fairness argument. While it may be a ridiculous public policy for the government to subsidize health insurance premiums for people who choose to retire early and reduce their income, that's the law of the land, just as it's the law of the land for the government to subsidize the medical costs of people who are older. When you're making a decision about how to live your life, it's not your responsibility to decide if the implications of public policy and existing laws are "fair" or "unfair." Your only responsibility is to make reasonable plans for the future based on the rules that are in place at the time; it's up to Congress to change unjust laws.

So, in short, if you're willing to make the tradeoffs necessary to quit the workforce decades earlier than usual, it's absolutely possible and there's nothing wrong with it. But working to age 70 is okay too as long as it's something you want and not something you're forced into by a wasteful spouse who really "needs" a 10th Louis Vuitton purse to go with her new Tesla.

What if you achieve your goals early?

Retirement accounts are really great. The only thing more exciting than stuffing money away for the future and getting a tax deferral in the process is watching someone else change the oil in your car. And in case you can't tell, I'm being sarcastic. Watching someone else change motor oil is really boring, and so is thinking about retirement accounts.

But retirement accounts still are really great even if they're boring too.

The power of tax-deferred, compound growth and the power of arbitraging the difference between the high tax brackets of your working years and the low tax brackets of your retirement years is enormous. The problem is that retirement accounts punish you with a 10% penalty, in addition to income taxes, if you take distributions before age 59 ½, and being unable to access your money or getting blasted with taxes rather takes the fun out of retiring at 45.

The good news is that there are several options open to early retirees which make it relatively easy to avoid the 10% penalty when accessing your retirement funds (unfortunately, your options to avoid the ordinary income taxes are about as limited as your options for marrying a supermodel).

<u>Asset swapping</u>. For people who have large, taxable investment portfolios in addition to their retirement portfolios, the easiest and most direct option for avoiding this penalty is asset swapping.

Let's say you receive $10,000 in dividends in your traditional IRA that you'd like to use to cover your living expenses. If you withdraw the money from your IRA, your 10% penalty is $1,000 on top of regular income taxes, which really stinks. So don't take the cash out of your IRA.

Instead, look at your taxable portfolio and sell $10,000 worth of stock. Immediately buy back the same stock in your traditional IRA.

Tada! You now have your stock in the traditional IRA instead of your taxable portfolio, which leaves your overall portfolio unchanged, and you also have $10,000 cash in your taxable portfolio, which you can withdraw and use whenever you want.

As long as you still have non-retirement investments, this strategy can be employed as often as you wish to extract cash from your retirement accounts. While you do have to be mindful of the impact of capital gains taxes, you can pick and choose positions to swap that minimize the tax. Even if you do have some capital-gains-tax expense, you won't owe ordinary income tax on the amount of assets swapped and you'll never owe penalties, so you'll likely come out ahead.

Over long periods of time, this strategy would have the effect of depleting your taxable investment portfolio while letting your retirement account grow untouched. Eventually, you'll have to take taxable retirement withdrawals, but if this strategy buys you enough time to make it to age 59 ½ and avoid penalties permanently, you're a winner.

Even without a taxable investment portfolio to swap out, there are four additional strategies you can use for accessing your retirement funds early.

Just pay the penalty. It's counterintuitive, but there are times when paying a penalty might not actually cost you much, if anything. Let's say you're married with two kids, and you earn $30,000 in annual, taxable dividends. You want to pull an additional $35,000 out of your IRA for the year.

Your dividends are taxed at the 0% bracket, so you don't even have to think about them. With a $24,800 standard deduction, the only regular tax you'll owe is 10% on $10,200 of your IRA withdrawal. The 10% early-withdrawal penalty of $3,500 brings your total tax bill to $4,520. However, with two children, you're entitled to a $4,000 child tax credit, leaving you with a net tax bill of only $520.

A tax of $520 is small enough that simply paying the penalty is no big deal in exchange for making life simple. If you don't expect your income to be very high, start by figuring out if just paying the tax might be your best bet.

72(t). The 72(t) section of the tax code is known as "substantially equal periodic payments" or "SEPP." This involves some fairly complex calculations involving your age, your beneficiary's age, reasonable interest rates, and your starting account balance. While the exact calculation is best done in consultation with your IRA trustee, the bottom line generally results in a distribution of 3% - 5% of your IRA balance that you take out each year without penalty.

Having regular access to your retirement money early and without penalty is great, but there is one big drawback to using this tool: You MUST take distributions each and every year until you turn 59 ½ (or until 5 years elapse, whichever is longer). If you fail to take even one distribution correctly, the IRS assesses a 10% penalty on EVERY distribution you took, retroactive to the start.

That sounds scary, and it is, so you don't want to enter into a 72(t)-distribution plan lightly. But if you're reasonably confident that you'll want to take out money from your IRA each year and that your plans aren't likely to change (e.g., you're not likely to go back to work), an annual, penalty-free distribution from your IRA makes early-retirement planning much easier. There's no reason to be afraid of this option.

Roth IRA conversion ladders. This is one of my favorite early-distribution-without-penalty strategies.

Since Roth IRAs are funded with after-tax dollars, you have the option to withdraw your original contributions at any time without tax or penalty. That's great, but if much of your money is locked up in a traditional IRA or 401(k), you might not have many Roth IRA contributions to withdraw.

The key to the Roth-IRA-conversion-ladder strategy is to realize that a Roth IRA conversion is treated like a contribution. You can withdraw converted money early and without penalty just like a contribution, which effectively makes your traditional IRA accessible at any time as long as you do a Roth IRA conversion first.

Of course, it's never that easy. There's a special rule requiring you to wait at least five years before withdrawing the original principal from a Roth conversion. But once that timer is exhausted, the money is ready and available at your convenience and without any penalties or additional taxes.

This is extremely powerful.

If you have the capacity to plan your cash flow at least five years in advance, you have effective access to as much of your retirement account as you want, whenever you want. The only limit is how much tax you want to pay each year on funds you convert from the traditional IRA to the Roth IRA, and you can make your tax as high or low as you think is reasonable by converting as much or as little money as you want.

The five-year rule applies separately to each Roth conversion you do, so it's helpful to look at an example. Let's assume you start with a $100,000 traditional IRA balance and a $0 Roth balance, you earn 7% per year on your money, and your goal is to withdraw $10,000 per year.

Year	Amount Converted	IRA Balance	Roth Balance	Roth Funds Available
0	$0	$100,000	$0	$0
1	$10,000	$90,000	$10,000	$0
2	$10,000	$86,300	$20,700	$0
3	$10,000	$82,341	$32,149	$0

4	$10,000	$78,105	$44,399	$0
5	$10,000	$73,572	$57,507	$10,000
6	$10,000	$68,722	$71,533	$20,000
7	$10,000	$63,533	$86,540	$30,000
8	$10,000	$57,980	$102,598	$40,000
9	$10,000	$52,039	$119,780	$50,000
10	$10,000	$45,681	$138,164	$60,000

Starting in year 1, you do a $10,000 Roth IRA conversion. Your traditional IRA balance goes down by $10,000, and your Roth IRA balance goes up by $10,000. No cash is available for withdrawal, yet, but you keep repeating this process each year.

Starting in year 5, the magic begins. The $10,000 you converted in year 1 is now available for withdrawal without income taxes and without penalties. In year 6, the $10,000 you converted in year 2 becomes available for withdrawal. In year 7, you can take out the $10,000 converted in year 3. And each year into the future, another $10,000 becomes available to withdraw from your Roth IRA.

If you don't need the money right away, you can let it compound, tax-free, until you need it. In this example, by year 10 you would have $60,000 available to withdraw any time you want with no tax and no penalty, which sure beats the large tax hit you'd take pulling $60,000 out of your traditional IRA all at once.

Although you have to pay income taxes each year on the money you convert to a Roth IRA, the tax bill isn't too big if you make small, annual conversions and if you're not working, and you don't actually have to withdraw the money in later years if you don't need it. But if you do need it, it's available, and that flexibility is very important for peace of mind.

<u>In-marriage QDRO</u>. QDRO stands for "Qualified Domestic Relations Order." These generally come up during divorces when spouses are splitting up certain types of retirement accounts, usually a 401(k). The tax code provides that if a couple is separating, there shouldn't be a penalty-tax event on the division of the retirement plan. While taxable distributions are subject to ordinary income taxes, there's no early-withdrawal penalty if a QDRO is in place and you pull money out of your 401(k) account to give to your spouse (different rules govern IRAs; this section relates to 401(k) plans only).

The funny thing, though, is that the tax code doesn't actually say anywhere that you have to get divorced in order for a judge to issue a QDRO and divide a 401(k) plan without penalty. You can get a QDRO and stay married, thus enabling you to pull money out of a 401(k) plan at will.

This is a bit of an exotic strategy, and it works best for large 401(k) withdrawals, but it's legal and it can be executed at any time with no waiting period or delay.

First, if your 401(k) balance isn't as much as you want to withdraw, or if you don't have a 401(k) plan, you should either establish your own 401(k) plan with the help of a bank or brokerage company, or you should roll over some of your traditional IRA balance into your existing 401(k) plan. There's no problem with an individual setting up a solo 401(k) plan; no formal business is required.

Second, you should consult a divorce attorney who is familiar with QDROs. If you find one who knows about the "in-marriage QDRO," that's even better, but it's not required.

Third, your attorney will help you to get a judge to approve the QDRO. The judge might be confused since you're not getting divorced, but he can still approve the order anyway.

Finally, you'll send the order to your 401(k) sponsor and withdraw the funds in your spouse's name, giving you penalty-free access to the money.

Setting up a 401(k) plan might cost you $1,000 - $2,000 if you don't have one already, and an attorney might cost you another $2,000 or $3,000. This isn't a cheap strategy, but if you're planning to make an early withdrawal of $100,000 or more from a retirement plan, paying $5,000 in legal and administrative fees is better than paying $10,000 in early-withdrawal penalties. Obviously, this makes more sense as you deal with larger numbers and the penalty you avoid becomes larger than the fixed fees, and it makes no sense at all if you want to make only a small withdrawal.

This strategy also makes the most sense for couples who have been married a long time and aren't particularly sentimental. Many newly-weds would scoff at the prospect of spending a lazy Saturday afternoon together down at the divorce-lawyer's office drafting ways to get a judge to split up their retirement plans. Long-married spouses who pursue this route also run the risk of finding out just how easy it is to get money from the other spouse and how easy it would be to get a divorce after so many years of putting up with you and your annoying habits, so tread with care.

CHAPTER 16: POTPOURRI

There's a curious product on the market. It consists of bits of trash stuffed in bags, and it's sold at home stores as "potpourri." Supposedly this desiccated debris is good for something, although what, exactly, I don't know, and while I'm told it has something to do with smells, the only smell I can detect is the smell of rotting yard waste. That's not exactly a smell I want in my home.

I don't pretend to understand why potpourri exists, and although I'll buy it if my wife tells me we "need" it, it's a product for which I have nothing but contempt and loathing.

So why did I name this chapter after an abomination? Because Jeopardy! named a category of miscellaneous questions after this offense against nature, and everyone needs a miscellaneous category.

Two-Income Families vs. One-Income Families

When my kids were in second grade, there was a parents' day. Each of the kids said a bit about what his parents did, and the parents could answer some questions from the kids. I can't tell you how often one of the little towheaded scamps would stand up and say, "my Mommy takes care of me and my family, but I really wish she'd leave and go to an office so I wouldn't have to spend time with her and she could buy me more toys."

The reason I can't tell you how often a kid said that is because no kid ever said that. Or at least no kid ever said that who didn't deserve to get punished for being ungrateful.

Guilt aside, there are quite a lot of factors that should be considered for a couple where one spouse is working and the other one might or might not work outside the home. Although this question involves money and most people view it as a money question, ironically, it's mostly a non-economic decision. You have to ask yourself:

1. Do you find fulfillment in working?
2. Is earning a paycheck something that makes you happy by itself, regardless of what you might do with the money?
3. Is there anything you can do with additional money that would make you happier?
4. If you have children, how would working outside the home impact them vs. having less money and spending more time with them?

5. Do you have any beliefs about traditional gender roles or childcare roles?
6. Do you have debt you to want pay (e.g., one spouse has student loans and doesn't want the other spouse to pay them)?
7. Do you have prior obligations to a workplace or prior financial obligations you need to settle?

These are questions with no right or wrong answer. These are lifestyle choices and value judgments that only you can answer. While the economic considerations might factor into the decision, they are still secondary. That doesn't mean they're unimportant, and you should still understand the effect of a second income on your family, but there are cases where a second income could cause a family to have less money, and if working full time caused you to have less money, would it still bring in enough personal fulfillment to make it worthwhile?

How do you have a job and become poorer? Thank the combination of progressive income taxes and costly childcare. Here's an example:

Jimmy is a workaholic neurologist. His favorite activities include running his neurology practice 80 hours per week, reading neurology journals, and neglecting his wife. He earns $400,000 per year, which his wife says he earns primarily by neglecting her.

Jimmy's wife Helga works full time as an office assistant. She earns $45,000 per year. But that's before taxes. Although a couple can choose to have some taxes withheld from one spouse and some taxes withheld from a second spouse, that's the wrong way to look at it.

Instead, you should have taxes withheld from the higher-earning spouse as if the second spouse didn't work at all, and the second spouse should have full, marginal taxes withheld. That's because the second income gets no additional deductions, exemptions, tax credits, or any other tax benefits, while simultaneously being stuck at the couple's highest tax bracket, and you need a clear understanding of just how little that second paycheck brings in.

In the case of a Jimmy and Helga earning $445,000 per year, the Federal income tax bracket is 35%. Social Security tax eats another 6.2%, Medicare taxes are 1.45%, and if the couple lives in California, say goodbye to another 11.3%. So, right off the bat Helga is losing 53.95%, or $24,277.50, just in direct taxes on her paycheck. Then she has to pay $11,800 per year for each of her two kids to go to daycare. Work clothes cost $3,000 per year, a second car for commuting costs $1,200 per year for gas, $1,000 per year for insurance, and $6,000 per year for car payments.

Helga is tired when she gets home, so she and her family eat out more often at a cost of $5,000 per year. And, of course, Helga doesn't want to clean the house after working, so she needs a housekeeper, but considering how much money Jimmy earns, he already paid for a housekeeper for Helga, so let's not count that against her.

When you add it all up, Helga earns $45,000, and she spends $59,077.50 to earn the income, for a net loss of $14,077.50 each year. That's money she loses working full time for someone else!

If she quit her job, her family would have more money and she would have more time. She chooses to take the loss and work anyway, however, because her boyfriend Gary also works at her office, and unlike that rotten Jimmy, he doesn't neglect her.

The exact variables that go into losing money from working differ from couple to couple, but broadly speaking, the bigger the difference in wages, the higher the marginal tax bill on the second income. If childcare and commuting expenses are high as well, then you are probably not making very much money from that second income, and you should sit down and figure out what is really left over at the end of the day.

For other couples where the pay rates are fairly close, particularly if there are no small children involved, the second income actually produces net income, which can be used to help you reach your financial goals faster, pay down debt faster, or increase the cost of your lifestyle. Those are all great financial reasons to work in addition to personal fulfillment, but there is a risk from lifestyle inflation.

If a couple builds a lifestyle that depends on two incomes, they are in a danger zone. Sometimes people lose jobs, for example, and the odds of someone losing a job at some point in the future go up significantly when both spouses are working. A single-income family faced with a job loss might counteract that by having the other spouse work for a while, but a dual-income family has far fewer options.

That dependency on a second income also ties your hands if you have kids down the road or want to make a lifestyle choice that involves less working. It's great to want to spend time with the new baby, but if you've got an extra-large mortgage because you wanted to get an extra bathroom for your house, coupled with two BMWs featuring his and hers car payments, you don't really have much choice in the matter.

Working or not working doesn't have to be an all-or-nothing decision. It's okay to change your mind if you don't like how things are going, and it's okay to work part-time instead of full time if that's something you want. Or you might consider earning two incomes while living on only one income and saving the rest, both to preserve flexibility for the future and to build your finances faster.

In the end, success in personal finance is all about having choices. People can disagree about what the right choices are, but you should never do anything that restricts your ability to make choices that are right for you.

Credit Scores

Once upon a time there was a happy little frog. The little frog had a wonderful credit score. With the help of his little frog wife, he used his credit to buy a happy little frog car, a happy little frog house, a happy little frog vacation, and tons and tons of happy little frog anime figurines.

Within a month, the happy little frog was inundated with debt and finance charges, and he spent the next 30 years giving 30% of the flies he caught to the government, 39% of the flies to his ex-wife who divorced him over his poor financial condition (which she helped create), and 30% to the banks to cover his frog finance charges. The happy little frog was no longer happy, despite his excellent credit score and record of on-time payments.

What can we learn from this unfortunate frog? Certainly, credit scores are important, but credit scores don't automatically make you happy. A credit score is just another tool in your financial toolkit. It can help you to get the best rates if you choose to borrow money, but by no means should it be viewed as an indication that you should borrow money. That is a completely separate question.

First: What is a credit score? Although there are several variations, all credit scores look at your history of dealing with payments and debt and assign a number to you that estimates the risk you won't meet your financial obligations in the future. Who doesn't enjoy being reduced to a number? The scale generally goes from 300 to 850, with ranges of:

300 – 579 -- Toxic waste
580 – 669 -- Probably won't pay
670 – 739 -- Good
740 – 799 -- Pretty safe
800 – 850 -- Heavenly.

If you're more likely to default on a payment or loan, a bank is less likely to lend you money, or if they do lend you money, they're likely to charge you a higher interest rate to compensate for the default risk. Thus, a stronger credit score makes it easier to get into debt on preferable terms. For example, someone with a very high credit score might get a personal loan from a bank at a 5% interest rate and a free cup of coffee when he visits his banker. Someone with a very low credit score might get a "personal" loan from Guido the loan shark at 25% per week with an option for broken legs if he misses a payment.

Very few major banks in the U.S. will break your legs if you miss a payment.

Second: What goes into a credit score? There are five main categories: payment history (35%), amount owed (30%), length of credit history (15%), new credit inquiries (10%) and credit mix (10%).

If you pay on time, you don't owe too much money, you have had credit over many years, you're not opening new accounts, and you have some credit cards and installment loans, then you'll probably get a great credit score.

Third: How do you keep your credit score high? There are a few basic rules to follow:

1. Always make at least the minimum payment on every debt you have. Late and missed payments can hurt you for years.

2. Keep your balances low as a percentage of your credit lines. Better yet, don't have any balances. This is more of a factor for revolving debt like credit cards than for mortgages, student loans, car loans, and other installment payments.

3. Keep your oldest credit card opened. That determines the length of your credit history. If you're young, open a credit card, even if you don't use it, so you can start the timer on the age of your credit history.

4. Don't apply for too many new credit lines if you expect to take on a major debt soon, like a mortgage or car loan. Generally, though, applications for new credit don't hurt you much after six months.

Some people think that carrying debt somehow helps your credit score, but it doesn't. Using a credit card for purchases and paying it off each month is better than having revolving balances. Carrying unnecessary debt serves only to generate finance charges for the bank.

That's really all there is to managing a credit score: good habits and time. The more of each you add in, the better your score. Credit repair services or other shortcuts that promise to turn a bad credit score into a good one are pie-in-the-sky scams that will separate you from your money. If you're inclined to go this route, let me know. I like pie.

Don't lend money to friends and relatives

Indiana Jones is an iconic hero who's great at swooping in and saving the day. I really liked the part where Indy was chasing after the Holy Grail, and a friend of his from the university came up to him and asked to borrow some money to help with his car payment since his wife was in the hospital after he recently lost his job. Indy handed the guy $500, saved the day, and never heard from his friend again.

As much as people want to be the hero, and as tempting as it is to step in and help friends and relatives in need, especially when all you have to do is write a check (metaphorically, of course; who uses checks?), you shouldn't do it.

A distant relative of mine once was asked how he became so wealthy. He answered that, "I never lend money to people. It's better that they should be angry at me while I have my money than that I should be angry at them while they have my money."

He was right. Under the best case, a friend or relative who borrows money from you pays you back. The vast majority of the time is not the best case, and if you lend money to someone, chances are you're never going to get it back and the relationship is going to be destroyed with anger and resentment. If you don't make the loan, the relationship could be destroyed with anger and resentment. If the relationship is going to be destroyed anyway, you might as well keep your money. But there are other reasons to avoid lending to friends and family.

People with bad financial habits who spend beyond their means, digging themselves into perpetual debt with no plan for the future, are actually not helped with additional loans. The loan might help cover a few bills or put off the day of reckoning, but the overspending will continue. Behavioral changes are the only way to make long-lasting improvements in your finances. Additional loans merely enable the bad behavior. Is your overspending-friend going to spend less because you gave him a loan, or is he just going to go on his merry way?

When he goes on his merry way, he'll probably mention to other people about your generosity. As your generosity increases, the number of needy friends and relatives you have increases proportionately. It's a remarkably consistent fact that when you help people based on need, the amount of "need" around you increases significantly.

Worse still, even if you bankrupt yourself giving away money to relatives and "friends," all the people you helped are going to forget you and disappear. The world is not It's a Wonderful Life. You won't find yourself in your own time of need down the road, only to be surprised in your darkest hour when all the people whose lives you improved with your generosity crowd around you, hand you a giant basket of money, and literally sing your praises. The only thing you can expect from your generosity is abandonment.

That said, if you really want to help someone, there is a less bad way to do it. To avoid resentment, any help you give you should be in the form of gifts, not loans. If you don't expect to be repaid, you won't have any resentment toward the person you helped, and the person you helped won't feel any pressure or embarrassment around you. Gifts are the only way to have a chance of maintaining a relationship, although if you're looking for an alternative, the best form of help comes from offering a job or contract or some other form of business opportunity, as you make it possible for the other person to help himself.

Also, you should concentrate your help on problems that are not recurring and that are not the fault of the person you're helping. For example, if a hard-working friend is injured in a car wreck and runs into financial trouble from being temporarily out of work and inundated with hospital bills, helping that person financially is okay. People won't seek out the opportunity to get into car wrecks again, and you're not enabling any kind of bad behavior with your help (although if your friend does seek out car wrecks, you might consider helping with the psychiatric bills).

If you know someone who has no car, and who, with the gift of an inexpensive car, could obtain employment that would otherwise be inaccessible, financial help is okay. Or if another friend is watching TV in his house when the sky opens up above him and a thunderous voice booms, "I am your Lord; you have failed to follow My 12th Commandment, and as was written in the Book of Bob the Pirate, one who fail to follow My 12th Commandment shall have 10% of his house destroyed," and if the insurance claim on the destruction of 10% of the house is subsequently denied under the "Act of God" clause in the insurance contract, it's okay to help financially since your friend didn't even have any warning that a 12th Commandment existed, and presumably won't repeat whatever behavior led to the destruction.

But if your friend loves to shop and can't afford to pay his credit card bills, giving your friend more money simply encourages additional overspending, and financial help should be avoided.

There's no one-size-fits-all answer for when it's okay to help people and when it's not, but the less at fault the person is for the loss and the less likely it is to recur, the more likely that helping would be beneficial instead of harmful.

Charitable giving

Ironically, giving money to strangers through charity is much less fraught with peril than giving money to friends and family. They're strangers, after all, and you have no relationship to destroy. If I got into a fight with the March of Dimes and they refused to talk to me ever again, I wouldn't exactly be broken up, nor would I be concerned about how awkward Thanksgiving dinner would be when the March of Dimes walked in and started badmouthing me to everyone else at the table.

But charitable giving comes with a very real danger: The charity might not stop talking to you. The generosity-begets-need dynamic is just as strong with charities as it is with individual people. Every time you give money to a charity, you get added to that charity's donor list, and they have very little incentive to take you off the list while they badger you incessantly for more money for their growing needs.

Worse yet, charities build their donor bases by exchanging lists of their donors for lists of donors from other similar charities and then contacting the other charity's donors. The hope is that each charity will get the other donors to give to them too, and it's not just a hope; it's a proven tactic that works based on decades of direct marketing experience.

If you give a gift to one organization one time, you could reasonably expect to be solicited by twenty other organizations. If you give gifts to more than one organization and if you give multiple times, you could get hundreds of solicitations. For people who like to donate often, it's not uncommon to receive bins of mail and hundreds of e-mails daily all begging for money. It can be overwhelming and enough to make you throw up your hands in despair.

The only way to avoid this is either by not giving to charity at all or by giving with a false name and address. Perhaps someone could fix this problem by starting a charity with a mission to rid the world of charitable solicitations. I'd be happy to contribute to such a cause, but I haven't yet because nobody solicited me.

People who hate solicitations probably won't give to charity anyway, but even people who don't mind the requests don't always want to donate money. Not everyone is charitably minded. There's nothing wrong with that.

On the other side, some religions make it a point that moral people should give away a portion of their money. Perhaps coincidentally, religious organizations are the biggest beneficiaries of their own moral decree to give, which seems like a conflict of interest, but no religious organization defines their own conflict of interest to be immoral, which is another handy coincidence. Of course, there's nothing wrong with giving to religious organizations if that's what you want to do.

How you prioritize charitable giving is a very personal topic without a right or wrong answer. It is more philosophical than mathematical.

My personal view is that any moral imperative to give is more than covered when the government takes 40% of your income to give away to other people, and if you want to help more people anyway, it's best to start with the needs of your immediate family before strangers, and it's best to help by giving jobs or business to help avoid dependency. But if you do want to give more money anyway, there are a few important things to keep in mind.

1. You should never hurt yourself by giving. If charitable activity is done at the expense of your other priorities (e.g., saving for retirement, paying off debts, making sure your kids have electricity, feeding your starving parents, filling your emergency fund, etc.), you can get yourself in trouble if you fall on hard times. It's great to give away 10% of your income, but if you run into hard times yourself, or if you're a little short on your retirement goals, the charities aren't going to be there to help you.

2. Even if you can afford it, you should never give away more than 20% of your income. Taking care of yourself

and your family and contributing capital for business investment is a virtue just as much as charitable giving.

3. Charitable giving is best reserved for later in life. When you're young and earning money, you have no idea what your future financial needs are going to be, or what risks you're going to face. If you run into a medical issue, job loss, divorce, or other catastrophe, it's important to have resources available to you (except for divorces; you don't want your soon-to-be ex, one of the most awful people in the world, to get half the money you intended to go to charity).

   When you're older and retired, after you've achieved your financial goals, you have a much clearer picture of your long-term needs and a safer idea of how much money you can distribute to others without jeopardizing your own future. You can even leave a generous gift out of your estate since you certainly won't need the money then. Don't feel guilty about not meeting charitable needs at a younger age; I guarantee you the future is going to have poverty and disasters too.

4. If you feel strongly that you should give when you're young, consider putting your charitable gifts into a separate investment account in your own name. If you run into financial trouble, you can always call upon that account for help. If you never run into financial trouble, the power of long-term investment growth and compound interest could leave you with a gigantic pot of money to distribute in your old age, thus making up for not giving earlier.

While on the topic of giving away money, I should mention leaving a legacy to your children while avoiding the estate tax. The amazing answer: Don't worry about it.

If you don't want to leave an inheritance for your kids, it's easy to spend everything. The kids are a bunch of ingrates who don't visit enough and who don't deserve your money. The more flamboyantly you can waste your money in front of them, the better.

Alternatively, if you like your kids and want to leave an inheritance for them, you can achieve that by following all the rules and recommendations for taking care of your own financial health, and the inheritance will naturally follow the failure of your physical health. And as for the estate tax, the current exemption is $23 million for a married couple, which covers just about everybody. If you have more than $23 million, you should consider getting estate planning advice from a source other than a book.

ABOUT THE AUTHOR

Joseph Metzger is a financial and investment consultant with twenty years of experience in finance, administration, and management, specializing in non-profit organizations, and thirty years of experience with investment management.

He goes by "Joe" to his friends, so most people call him "Mr. Metzger." Mr. Metzger enjoys various hobbies, including spreadsheets, personal finance reading, reviewing tax laws, and filling out government paperwork.

Mr. Metzger lives in Virginia with his wife and two daughters and can be reached at MetzgerPublishing@Gmail.com.

www.ingramcontent.com/pod-product-compliance
Lightning Source LLC
Chambersburg PA
CBHW052346220526
45465CB00003BA/978